A Whole New World

Great insights
into transformation
and togetherness

The Gospel of Mark

John Blackwell

Morgan James Publishing • NEW YORK

A Whole New World

Great insights into transformation and togetherness
The Gospel of Mark

John Blackwell
Copyright ©2007 John Blackwell

ISBN-13: 978-1-60037-159-2 (Hardcover)
ISBN-13: 978-1-60037-158-5 (Paperback)
ISBN-13: 978-1-60037-229-2 (eBook)
ISBN-13: 978-1-60037-231-5 (Audio)

Published by:

MORGAN · JAMES
THE ENTREPRENEURIAL PUBLISHER™
www.morganjamespublishing.com

Morgan James Publishing, LLC
1225 Franklin Ave Ste 32
Garden City, NY 11530-1693
Toll Free 800-485-4943
www.MorganJamesPublishing.com

Cover/Interior Design by:
Rachel Campbell
rcampbell77@cox.net

Habitat for Humanity®
Peninsula
Building Partner

Dedication

To Jim Standiford

Colleague and Friend

With the deepest of gratitude

Table of Contents

Foreword
BY KYRA PHILLIPS

WHEN THE REVEREND DR. JOHN BLACKWELL ASKED me in the Fall of 2005 to be the 2006 commencement speaker at Kansas Wesleyan University, I thought God just wanted me to inspire a graduating class. I was wrong. There was a much bigger plan. God was about to put me back in school, teaching me a life lesson that would not only graduate me to the next level in my personal and spiritual walk, but also inspire me in ways I never knew or even thought I needed.

Not knowing it at the time, I was about to embark on a personal transformation through the Gospel of Mark, thanks to Dr. Blackwell.

This journey began in Salina, Kansas, as I was getting ready for the KWU commencement address. I had been riding an emotional and spiritual rollercoaster for a couple of years and had not been very good at extending myself much grace. Guilt, confusion, and inner conflict had all been building up in my head and heart for some time. Like many people, I was searching for answers and for peace of mind. Part of that search included a question that I posed to Dr. Blackwell: "Do you ever wrestle with demons?" I remember his face with such clarity. His eyes were curious; he wanted to inquire more, and his analytical side was going into overtime. I felt I struck a chord with the man and the pastor that my parents have always referred to as "A philosophical intellect."

"Kyra," he said, "we all wrestle with demons." What a relief, I thought. I wasn't alone! I was just another one of God's children looking and searching for resolution—for the clarity that would quell my restless heart, head, and spirit.

I never realized that one of the major themes in the Gospel of Mark is about learning to see clearly. The Gospel invites us to be curious, to wonder, to embrace mystery, to listen, to absorb, to see the actions of Jesus and blend them into our lives. A big part of that understanding is to confront our demons and confront them head-on. Dr. Blackwell teaches, "The most important learning involves the places where I am the weakest." It's not easy for us to admit that we often need to cleanse our souls, but we can do it through the power of God and his Grace.

Dr. Blackwell writes about the things that are revealed in this Gospel through eyes that recognize our demons. Just as Mark describes the scene where Jesus calms the sea, Jesus also can deliver us from that ever so common uproar in our souls! Dr. Blackwell strongly believes that the best people who have lived have faced the demons within. I couldn't agree more. We must be humble, acknowledge our inner conflicts, be self-reflective, embrace the good and evil in each one of us, and then endure the mystery of self-discovery, thus allowing ourselves to be transformed.

So where do we begin? Dr. Blackwell lays it out beautifully in his book by describing how three complementary phases—recognition, interpretation and reflection, and implementation—can work for us.

This book was ministry, a gift, and a soul-tugging read. I challenge you to read this book and become spiritually transformed. Study the metaphors, the poetry, the lessons of our Messiah's ministry through Dr. Blackwell's interpretation and text. You will, without a doubt, embark upon "A Whole New World" and be peacefully enlightened.

Chapter 1

right before our eyes

*Oh, music's all very well. You know I love it. And any-
body can write; it just takes industry. But painting—it
makes people see. It makes them see God's work truly. .
. . The painter is a great moral force, Frankie. It's truly a
gift of God.* —Aunt Mary-Ben,
in Robertson Davies' *What's Bred in the Bone*

*The novelist must be characterized not by his function but
by his vision, and we must remember that his vision has to
be transmitted and that the limitations and blind spots of
his audience will very definitely affect the way he is able to
show what he sees.* —Flannery O'Connor,
"The Grotesque in Southern Fiction"

Can you see anything? —Jesus, in Mark 8:23 (NRSV)

I decided to take up drawing. It was something I had thought about
doing for years. A friend recommended that I use a book by Betty
Edwards, entitled *Drawing on the Right Side of the Brain*. I was intrigued
by the title. Among other things, Edwards shows us how, as we learn to
draw, we let the right side of the brain take over, so to speak, and show
us untold riches.

It was in beginning to learn to draw that I realized how little I actually see. Learning to draw has as much to do with seeing what is right
in front of me as with skill. Betty Edwards gives wonderful exercises to

1

improve necessary drawing skills, to be sure. But the most important feature of drawing involves seeing. To learn to draw well, we have to learn to see well. When I started reading Edwards' book and actually doing some of her exercises, I realized just how poorly I saw. I discovered how little attention I actually paid to what was right in front of my nose and eyes!

The awareness of how little I actually see didn't come as a surprise. There is a famous test that is called the *Myers-Briggs Personality Inventory*. The purpose of this inventory is to give us insight into some of our preferred ways of functioning. One of the categories has to do with how we go about gathering information. The idea is that we tend to rely either on our senses or our intuition. Those who prefer to sense things like to acquire information through seeing, hearing, tasting, touching, and smelling. In other words, sensors prefer to sense things. It's just that simple.

Instead of the senses, others prefer their intuition. People who rely on intuition like to discern the unseen—what can be known, so to speak, through the mind's eye. This is where I fit in. The last time I took the *Myers-Briggs* test, all of my answers indicated a preference for intuition. I got no points for sensing.

This isn't helpful when it comes to learning to draw! I tend to be comfortable in the inner world of ideas. One of my problems is that it is so easy for me to withdraw into the world of intuition and ideas that I can get lost there. When I do so, I am absent from the real world. My children tell me that they can always recognize when I am off in the world of my own intuition. They say that I begin staring off into space—both literally and figuratively.

There's nothing wrong with this—to a point. The world of intuition and ideas is important, as is the world of things. But as I began to learn to draw, I also discovered a weakness. There is much that I never see. Rarely do I look intently at what is right before my eyes. Too often, I'm gone to the world. If I was to begin to learn to draw, I would have to begin to learn to see what was right in front of me.

This is one of the major themes of Mark's Gospel. Mark is all about learning to see clearly. One of Mark's goals was to teach his reader to see. Mark accomplished this by showing us what he saw. That's why he wrote his Gospel in the first place. Mark wanted to show us what he saw when he looked at Christ. He also wanted to show us what Christ saw when he looked at the world. Mark's ultimate goal was to open our eyes so that we could see the world that is right before our eyes, recognizing the Christ who is right in front of us. In a word, Mark's Gospel is all about insight. His Gospel is the embodiment of his own insight.

From childhood, I remember the words, "Now you see it. Now, you don't!" This was a standard phrase used by magicians. The technical word for this kind of "magic" is *prestidigitation*. Using slight of hand, the magician would make an object disappear—right before our eyes. For years, I found magic associated with slight-of-hand electrifying. I was enchanted with what Robertson Davies calls the *World of Wonders*.

Mark's Gospel is characterized not by the words, "Now you see it. Now, you don't," but by a beloved line from a hymn: "Was blind, but now I see." Mark wasn't interested in slight-of-hand, nor did he seek to make things disappear. He wasn't even interested in *making* Christ appear right before our eyes. He was interested in opening our eyes, teaching us to see. To this end, Mark took great care to show us what he himself saw.

To help us see what is right before our eyes, Mark spent considerable time on description. He took great care to portray the *actions* of Jesus. He wanted us to learn to see what Jesus was up to in his interactions with others. Some of these actions were startling. None were more so than his dealings with the blind man in the middle of chapter eight. I've heard more than one poet use the phrase, "God is in the details." In this story, the details are remarkable, and I find two of them to be strange, odd, and even puzzling. If we are reading with half a mind, we will at least pause and wonder: Why did Jesus do that? And if we will linger in our perplexity, it will lead to the even more important question: What is Mark showing us? What does he want us to see?

There is nothing remarkable about the way the story begins. Jesus and his disciples had just arrived at Bethsaida, and a group of people brought a blind man to Jesus, begging him to touch the man. Jesus's response was simple and direct. He took the man by the hand and led him from the village. This is something we might expect. In the first chapter of the Gospel, when Jesus called his first disciples, he said, "Follow me!" Discipleship involves learning to follow Christ. By portraying Jesus taking the blind man and leading him away from the village, Mark has shown us that learning to see goes hand-in-hand with following Jesus. Notice the subtlety with which Mark has accomplished this. He didn't portray Jesus lecturing the lad: "Now, Son, learning to see means following me, so I want you to take my hand and follow. We'll do this together, but I don't want you lagging behind. Any questions? Good. Ready? Let's go!" Instead, Mark's Gospel shows us Jesus responding to their request that he touch the man. Mark even shows the touch as it unfolds: Jesus took the hand of the blind man and led him away from the village.

I find this intriguing. Why did Jesus lead the man *away* from the village? Mark offered no explanation. But he did place the answer right before our eyes. The village is where the people gather. Does learning to see begin with being removed from the crowd? Does the crowd have a way of looking at things that is distorted, or skewed? How many times do we miss seeing what is really in front of us because we expect to see what we have been conditioned to see? Or how many times have we failed to see because we have depended on others to do our looking for us? It's hard for me to imagine that Jesus was removing the man from the village permanently, but getting away from crowds, clutter, and complicating confusions may be a necessary first step for Christ to open our eyes.

If I find Jesus's leading the man from the village to be intriguing, I find what Jesus does next to be astonishing. Jesus spits in the man's eyes. I am not surprised that the New Revised Standard Version softened what Mark wrote by making it less graphic and tasteless. This translation says that Jesus "put saliva on [the man's] eyes." But the Greek doesn't say that. There is nothing euphemistic in Mark's description. Jesus spat on his eyes. Mark was blunt, but he was blunt for a reason. Mark wrote with clear purpose. He had an end in his sights, and that end involves our ability to discriminate and understand the meaning of Jesus's actions in dealing with the blind man. In other words, he is interested in enlarging our capacity for insight—both as we look at Jesus's dealings with his circumstances and as we look at our own.

Before we look at the more difficult issue of why Jesus spat on the eyes of the blind man, I'd like to focus on an aspect of the story that is a bit less baffling. After spitting on the man's eyes, Jesus then laid his hands on the man and asked, "Can you see anything?" The man told Jesus, "I can see people, but they look like trees that are walking." His vision wasn't yet clear. Jesus then touched the man's eyes a second time. Finally, he could see. He looked intently. He saw clearly.

At the conclusion of this episode, Jesus admonished the man to stay away from the village. Jesus didn't want him to return immediately. This final admonition goes hand in hand with the unfolding of the man's eyesight. Learning to see takes time. In Mark's Gospel, time is essential. This is why the man's healing wasn't instantaneous. After Jesus first touched the man's eyes, *some* vision emerged, but he couldn't see clearly. His vision wasn't yet discriminating. He still lacked insight. Something more would have to happen for him to become fully and habitually perceptive and discerning. It was important for the man to remain apart from the ways in which his acquaintances customarily viewed the world if his own capacity for insight was to become second nature. He would have to learn to see what was right in front of his eyes as a matter of everyday intention.

What was right in front of his eyes at that moment was Jesus's spittle. This was what Jesus wanted him to see; and this, of course, brings us back to the puzzle: Why did Jesus spit in his eyes? I wish there were a nicer way to ask this question. I don't wish to give offense. The challenge is that there is nothing pleasant about this part of the story, and I can't find a more acceptable alternative. So we have to ask, what does Jesus's spitting on the eyes of the blind man—whom he is healing—have to do with gaining insight? To answer this most important question, we have only to ask, where else, in Mark's Gospel, do we see someone being spat upon? The answer, of course, is that Jesus himself was spat upon when he was on trial before the high priest in the temple.

This, in turn, leads to the question, why was Jesus put on trial? What was Jesus charged with? Of what was he convicted? He was charged with being the Messiah—the King of the Jews. When Pilate, the Roman governor, ordered Jesus to be crucified, the charge against him was posted: King of the Jews.

This is a curious charge. The people didn't deny that he was the Messiah. But some of the people spat on him. Why? One of their reasons was that Jesus didn't fit their idea of what a Messiah should be and do. They spat on him because they held this *kind* of Messiah in contempt. Some of the people had nothing but disdain for Jesus and the type of king he chose to be.

Jesus answered God's call to be the Messiah willingly. But after years of thoughtful deliberation, he wasn't willing to present himself as a military Messiah—a mighty warrior like the great King David, who would lead his followers in a great battle against the Roman occupiers of Jerusalem. Jesus had concluded that a military Messiah wasn't what the people needed and wouldn't serve the interests of the kingdom of God—the world of God's sovereignty. But if Jesus wouldn't lead his followers into battle, neither would he flee—withdrawing to the hills for a life of seclusion, isolation, and prayer. Instead, he would confront evil and confront it head-on, seeking somehow to take it all in—to absorb it into his own person. He would confront evil by embracing those who held him in contempt. He would confront evil by accepting those who rejected him. He would confront evil by offering hospitality to people who had been banished and left to the margins of society—women, lepers, sinners, tax collectors, and those possessed by evil. And, he would confront evil also by embracing those who had marginalized others—all of which would lead to his suffering. He would confront evil by means of his own suffering and death.

Jesus was spat upon by people who objected to a Messiah who embraced people whom they had banished from society and sent into exile. And this raises the important question, why would Jesus as Messiah *willingly suffer* rejection and a most cruel, excruciating death? I think it has to do with the *ends* for which Jesus was called, and for which he stood. The end for which Jesus stood was the peace of God. Domination isn't the means to peace. Consequently, Jesus carefully avoided dominating others. He sought peace. He didn't pound others into submission. He sought the life-giving peace of God's sovereignty and love.

To establish a world of firm peace and love takes time. The implementation of peace sometimes involves sacrifice. A Messiah who made sacrifice and even expected that his followers would do likewise was not the type of Messiah that many people wanted. Several in authority rejected Jesus. They rejected the *kind* of Messiah Jesus chose to be. These people held Jesus and the kingdom for which he stood in contempt. They expressed their contempt with the greatest of disdain. They spat on Jesus.

This is what Mark wanted us to see. He wanted us to observe Christ as he willingly embraced the people who held him in contempt. He wanted us to see Christ embracing the ones who rejected him. This is where we will find the sovereignty of God. This is what Mark wanted to help us recognize. Mark knew that if we were to see Christ embracing those whom he encounters, our own capacity for love and peace would grow larger. As we watch Christ embrace those who rejected him, Christ would also open our eyes to the people we might embrace in love.

Mark understood that this would not be easy. Christ's own disciples had great difficulty learning to see. At the very moment when Christ was embracing people who counted him as the enemy, his own disciples abandoned him and dissociated themselves from him. For Christ's disciples to recognize the significance of the way he embraced others would take time. I think that Mark understood that it will take time for those of us who read his Gospel to learn to see as well.

There is a lot to see in Mark's Gospel. Learning to see—especially in the initial phases—takes effort and time. Mark didn't deny the possibility that we will have flashes of insight. The challenge is that flashes can be difficult to sustain. Embracing and implementing insight takes time because it is a matter of learning. And for me, the most important learning involves the places where I am the weakest. The weak places are where I need the most learning and growth.

As I began learning to draw, one of the things that first struck me was that I would have to move my eyes slowly and then move the pencil slowly as well. As I began to slow down my efforts to draw, I also became aware of how rapidly I tended to move the pen when I wrote. I discovered this to be one of the reasons my penmanship was so poor (sloppy is the better characterization!). I then recognized that my penmanship was poor because my attention raced to the next topic of interest. I was too easily bored. This in turn led me to recognize how quickly I came to conclusions and how hastily I was wont to act. I also became aware that it was difficult for me to allow one enterprise to come to conclusion or completion because I was already looking forward to the next.

As I forced myself to slow down the pencil, I began to give impatience permission to relax its grip on my life. I began to give anxiety permission to let go. I also began to allow myself to take a more relaxed interest and sustained attention to what was right in front of me.

A favorite character from the world of literature is the creation of the remarkable imagination of the nineteenth century Russian novelist Fyodor Dostoevsky. The character is Father Zossima, an Orthodox monk. In a rather lengthy section, Father Zossima tried to help the other monks to make a connection between the material world that we see with the spiritual world that we intuit. This is a matter of learning to pay attention to what is right before our eyes and to make the appropriate connections to our life in God.

I am still learning to do this with consistency. It is a discipline that is difficult to sustain. I find it easier to do so while on retreat. One of my favorite retreats is St. Deiniol's Library in Wales. St. Deiniol's is a writer's paradise. The library is the legacy of the nineteenth century British Prime Minister William Gladstone. He wanted to insure that scholars and clergy had a place to read, reflect, and write. The result was this amazing residential library in the town of Hawarden.

When I am on retreat and actively pay attention, I notice the kinds of connections that Father Zossima speaks of—a connection between my thoughts and what is actually happening in the library. In years past, I have noticed that during those times when I ponder how it is that God is working to cleanse my soul, I will hear the sound of the cleaning lady working the vacuum. Here in Britain, they call it *Hoovering*—converting a brand name of a particular vacuum cleaner into a verb. The synchronous sound of the vacuum cleaner at the moment when I reflect on the cleansing of my soul evokes the concrete intuition that God is present in this library cleansing my soul from the sin of which I am conscious as I write.

I like to write on the second floor of the library. There are tables which, because they are surrounded by books, are quite private. Moreover, we are permitted to leave our books and study materials on the table on which we work, giving us a personal working space for the duration of our stay.

On the first day of my arrival for three weeks of writing, I staked out a library table, plugged in my laptop, and set to work. When I returned to my table on the second day, I discovered that the cleaning lady was sweeping the second floor, and as I approached the table where I would be working for the next three weeks, she was sweeping right under and around my table. What was happening here? God was opening my eyes. God was helping me to recognize that as I was on retreat, as I wrote, God was pouring grace into my life and cleansing my soul right where I was. As I was aware of my surroundings, as I pondered Mark's Gospel, as I reflected on my own soul and the circumstances of my own life, God was present, cleansing my life. The challenge was to see—to witness—that grace. The challenge was to *recognize* the presence of grace *right where I was*. This is the beginning of transformation. These are the first inklings of fulfillment—to begin to recognize God—the Presence of the Genuine—right where we are.

For Reflection

What kinds of things are right in front of me that I have failed to see? What difference would seeing make?

_____

_____

_____

What kinds of blinders do I wear? What are my obstacles to recognition?

_____

_____

_____

If someone were to describe my interactions with others, what would he or she see? What kind of role do I habitually play in my dealings with others? What kinds of results do my actions produce?

_____

_____

_____

At times, learning to see begins as we retreat (temporarily withdraw) from circumstances for reflection. What kind of retreat would benefit me? What am I willing to do about it?

_____

_____

_____

What is my reaction to a Christ who avoids dominating others? What role does domination play in my life?

_____

_____

_____

What kinds of things do I do to implement peace? What actions might I take?

_____

_____

_____

How am I when it comes to patience—taking enough time for growth to unfold in my life?

_____

_____

_____

How am I when it comes to embracing those who hold me in contempt? Is this a risk I am willing to take?

_____

_____

_____

Chapter 2

Jesus's first words

The time is fulfilled, and the kingdom of God has come near; repent, and believe in the good news.

— Jesus, in Mark 1:15 (NRSV)

These people in the invisible Church make discoveries that have meaning for us who are better protected from the vicissitudes of our own natures, and who are often too lazy and satisfied to make any discoveries at all.

— Flannery O'Connor,
"The Catholic Novelist in the Protestant South"

It was the summer of 1998. I was sitting in a classroom at Wadham College at the University of Oxford. The occasion was a summer institute in religious studies. The distinguished Scottish theologian John Macquarrie was giving a lecture. During the lecture, he made a side comment. It wasn't central to Macquarrie's topic, but it caught my attention. He said that it might be interesting to pay attention to the first words that Jesus speaks in each of the four Gospels. Macquarrie suggested that perhaps each of the Gospel writers selected Jesus's first spoken words deliberately. They may have everything to do with the purpose of each Gospel. Jesus's first words may hold the key to understanding what each of the writers wanted to accomplish.

I was intrigued by Macquarrie's suggestion. I had wanted to understand what each Gospel writer was up to. What were the Gospel writer's particular insights? What did each writer see? What was each Gospel writer witness to? I had also been thinking that an author's *purpose* in writing was important for many reasons, one of which was my hope that this might provide a way of understanding Scripture that would unite and transform us. I had been thinking that much of the division in our culture over the inspiration of scripture was needless. On the one hand, I knew devoted Christians who recognized that the Word of God merits reverence. The idea of somehow deconstructing Holy Scripture and tearing things apart was at best offensive to their sentiments and at worst blasphemous. On the other hand, I knew people of an intellectual bent who reacted rather strongly against a reading of Scripture that smacks of literalism. These people tended to be aware of the metaphors and poetry in the Bible. It seemed to me that both positions represented something important in our approach to the Bible.

But I also thought that the extreme positions weren't particularly helpful. On the one hand, it seemed that those proposing a literalistic approach were not truly literalistic. Whether we admit it or not, we are all aware, at some level, that the Bible contains metaphors. The first book in this series was on the Gospel of John. His is the easiest when it comes to spotting metaphors. When Jesus says, "I am the light of the world," none of us takes that literally. We don't think of Jesus as a photon of light, beaming through the universe at 186,000 miles per second. We do, on the other hand, recognize that Jesus evokes God's first words, "Let there be light." We also recognize that Jesus claims to be the one who lights the way for us to see and know God. Similarly, when Jesus says, "I am the door," we know that he isn't suggesting that he is made of wood and has a knob or a latch. He is saying that he is the way to God, or the way that we enter the kingdom of heaven. When Jesus says, "I am the good shepherd," he isn't claiming that he makes a living tending sheep. And when Jesus says, "I am the vine, and you are the branches," he is helping us to understand that through him we have a connection to each other and God, which we deny not only at peril to our souls, but to our life together as well. I would guess that almost all of us read *some* of the Bible as metaphor whether we think about it or not. And many of us recognize that where there are metaphors, they are quite powerful. The metaphors do something to us. They enter our souls through our imaginations. They somehow shape our thinking and transform our consciousness.

At the same time, I was finding that those who wanted to reduce the Bible to *mere* metaphor were not entirely responsible in their approach either. Many were reducing the Bible to fiction. It was *great* literature, to be sure, but it was something to be read *solely* as literature. Because the Bible could not be taken literally, and because there was little historical fact represented in the Bible, it might be more or less inspiring, but its authority was suspect. And the "believer" was free to pick and choose what to believe. One of the things that struck me odd about those who wished to fictionalize the Bible was that many seemed to be practicing a kind of fundamentalism. Perhaps without meaning to, they appeared trapped in what we might call a *secular fundamentalism*, or a fundamentalism of secularity. On the one hand, the mantra of these readers is *tolerance*. It is a buzzword. By championing tolerance, they were calling rather loudly for cultural diversity. The problem was that I wasn't finding much diversity in their approach to scripture, and I didn't hear much tolerance for those who interpreted the scripture differently. I was hearing even less tolerance for God's power for deliverance and transformation.

I have overstated the situation, painting in brushstrokes that are broad. But I have done so to raise a question: Is there a way for us to read the Bible *together* that expresses *both* deep reverence for God and respect for the sanctity of Scripture on the one hand *and* that is responsible in recognizing metaphor and history on the other?

As I sat listening to John Macquarrie, it occurred to me that by looking at Jesus's first words in the Gospels, we might find a key to understanding each Gospel's *purpose* and for seeing what each writer was witness to.

In Mark's Gospel, Jesus speaks his first words in the first chapter. This Gospel is packed with action. Things move quickly. When Jesus first appears, John baptizes Jesus in the Jordan River. Immediately after his baptism, Jesus spends forty days in the wilderness, where Satan puts him to the test. Mark wastes no time in telling us that Jesus's ministry will involve a battle for the kingdom of God—God's ultimate sovereignty.

At the conclusion of this temptation episode, Mark announces the arrest of John the Baptist. And at this precise moment, Jesus goes to Galilee and proclaims the Good News, saying, "The *time* is fulfilled, and the kingdom of God has come near; repent, and believe in the gospel." These are the first words of Jesus in the Gospel of Mark. When I first pondered the reasons why these words come first, I wrote some questions: Is Mark's entire Gospel about the fulfillment of time? If so, what does it mean to speak of the fullness of time? What does the fullness of time have to do with the nearness of God's kingdom—the world of God's unconditional sovereignty? And finally, what is this Good News, and what does it mean to believe in it?

Everything Mark says in these opening chapters is occupied with time. Mark uses the word "immediately" with frequency and urgency. We get an even clearer sense of this in Greek (the word Mark uses is *euthús*). When Jesus is baptized, as he rises up out of the water, *immediately* the heavens split open. At the conclusion of Jesus's baptism, he is *immediately* driven into the wilderness, where he is tempted. In the next episode, Jesus calls Simon and Andrew and James and John to follow him. Each set of brothers does so *immediately*. In the next episode, Jesus confronts a demon. When Jesus commands the demon to come out, the demon leaves the man *immediately*. Jesus and his disciples then leave the synagogue for Simon Peter's house *immediately*. Peter's mother-in-law is ill, and they tell Jesus *immediately*. Jesus then takes the woman by the hand and raises her up, and the fever leaves her *immediately*. And in the final episode of the first chapter, a leper approaches Jesus and requests that Jesus heal him. Willing to do so, Jesus touches the leper, and the leprosy leaves the man *immediately*. Jesus then charges the man with silence and sends him away *immediately*.

Mark uses the term nine times in this first chapter, and he doesn't stop using it there. What we notice is that throughout Mark's entire Gospel, time is of the essence. Mark conveys a clear sense of *urgency*. If not haste, we sense pressure and agitation from the outset. Things happen far more rapidly in Mark's Gospel than in the others. Jesus's first words in Mark come earlier than in any of the other three Gospels.

When Jesus announces the *fullness of time*, he refers to a particular quality of time. He doesn't speak of *chronos*, the word for chronological time. *Chronos* is linear time, the ordinary time of everyday occurrences. This is the time we measure—clock-time. *Chronos* is the time we're aware of when we're behind schedule. When Jesus announces the fullness of time, instead of using *chronos*, he uses *kairós*. *Kairós* has less to do with a quantity of time and more to do with a *quality of time*. *Kairós* isn't the linear time that we measure. It is the time that is pregnant with opportunities and possibilities. *Kairós* is the time that is ripe. With *kairós*, significant events from the past, along with possibilities from the future, are miraculously present. Those who understand this enjoy a new awareness of remarkable opportunity.

In July of 2003, Nancy and I celebrated our thirtieth wedding anniversary. When we celebrate, we like to keep things quiet and simple. We both do far better with small groups of people than with parties and other large gatherings. So we spent our anniversary alone—just the two of us. I took her to dinner at a lovely restaurant on the shore of the San Diego Harbor. Nancy loves cut flowers, so I arranged for a surprise. I ordered 30 long-stem red roses, which were on our bayside table when we arrived. I may never fully understand how much those flowers meant to her. Throughout our meal, she would occasionally say, "The flowers just blow me away."

What happened during the meal was an experience of *kairós*. We began to reflect. We began to remember. Nancy recalled our first date. It was on December 1, 1972. I took her to dinner at another restaurant on the harbor. She remembered what I was wearing. Other times from our past became present. Some were difficult. A few were even painful at the time. But on that July evening in 2003, we were able to remember fondly, to laugh, and even to marvel that we had made it as far as we have. We also began to talk about the future. We have no idea what the future holds. But we were aware that *right there, in that restaurant, at that table, our past and our future were mingled with our present*. That's the kind of thing Mark is talking about when he speaks of *kairós*. In a remarkable way, the past, and sometimes even the future, are present; they are there to be recognized.

Kairós is a remarkable reality. To understand the idea of *kairós*, I found the thinking of St. Augustine (354–430) to be helpful. His ideas on *time* are simple and ingenious. When he was asked how we know that time exists, St. Augustine said, "Because we measure it." In other words, it is self-evident that we would *not* measure something that did not exist because we *could not* measure it. He was then asked where time comes from. His answer was remarkable for its cleverness. He said that time comes from the future, which does not yet exist; it passes through the present, which has no duration, and into the past, which no longer exists.

This, of course, describes *chronos*, which is chronological time. But St. Augustine's description of chronological time helps us to understand what Mark means by *kairós*. *Kairós* is a quality of time that involves several things simultaneously. It first involves recalling the past into the present. This means that *kairos* draws what no longer exists into the present moment. In the present moment, which normally has no duration, the past is now miraculously sustained. At the same moment, a part of the future, which does not yet exist, also breaks into the present, where it is synchronized with the past, here and now. To put all of this together, *kairós* involves recalling the past, which no longer exists, and the future, which does not yet exist, into the present, which normally has no duration. The past and the future are sustained in the present. They are in sync with each other. And when particular parts of the past and the future are sustained and in sync, here and now, time becomes ripe and opportunities become golden. Time, which normally merely passes, becomes abundantly fruitful. Certain events, results, and outcomes become more likely. And this is because important events from the past and the future are remarkably present here and now.

Kairós is a quality of time in which the transformation of human life is teeming with possibilities. *Kairós* is the quality of time during which fulfillment comes to fruition. One of the illusions under which I labored for years involved the idea that fulfillment is usually instantaneous. I am not claiming that transformation and fulfillment never happen instantly, but Mark's insight is that they unfold in time. Transformation and fulfillment aren't so much akin to magic as they are to learning. Human learning—the kind that produces fruitful, lasting, productive, satisfying results—seems to unfold in what we might call three complementary phases. The first phase of transformation involves *recognition*—learning to see what's really happening right where we are, right before our eyes, right in the very circumstances in which we actually live. This is the kind of thing that happens in the first seven and a half chapters of Mark's Gospel (1:1—8:21). In these first chapters, Mark has us engaged in the challenge of recognizing the presence, meaning, and significance of grace and the power of God both in the impact that Jesus makes as he interacts with people and, by analogy, in the circumstances of our own lives.

The second phase of transformation involves what we might call *interpretation and reflection*. This is the kind of work that we do on retreats, in dialogue, in seclusion, in study, through journal writing, and as we actively reflect. Reflection involves learning to interpret, with sufficient thoroughness, using analogy: How is it that my own life and circumstances are *similar* to what we find, for example, in Mark's Gospel, and how is it that my own life and circumstances are different? How have I been living and responding to the mystery of life; and how will I respond to the mystery of life, given what I am learning? In the middle section of Mark's Gospel (8:21—10:52), Jesus carefully and painstakingly *interprets* for his disciples the movement of the power of God in his own life and ministry. This section renders this important part of human transformation so that it comes to fill our imaginations with remarkable possibilities for fulfillment.

The third phase of human transformation brings fulfillment to completion—*implementation*. Implementation involves taking the fruits of our careful reflections and living with deliberate forethought and insight. Implementation involves execution and performance. Implementation is the exercise of human will. It involves deliberate choice. Implementation is what brings the fruits of our reflection to fulfillment. In Mark's Gospel, Jesus wants us to recognize and to understand (through reflection) the realm and nature of God's call, sovereignty, and power. He wants us to understand not only *that* Jesus is the Messiah, but also *what kind* of Messiah Jesus is. Mark wants us to begin to visualize what the world of God's sovereignty looks like. This all comes to fruition when Jesus *implements* his own vision and understanding of the kingdom of God—the world of God's sovereignty. This is what unfolds in the final six chapters of the Gospel (chapters 11–16).

What Mark ultimately hopes that we will see is that the time for the beginning of our own transformation and fulfillment is right here, right now—in our very own circumstances. Now is the time! Now is the time to recognize the world of God's sovereignty. Now is the time to begin to understand the nature of God's power to deliver us. Now is the time to see what is right before our eyes. Now is the time to say yes to the power of God to transform us and to bring our lives to their genuine fulfillment.

For Reflection

What has been my attitude towards reading the Bible? How has my attitude helped me? How has it served as a roadblock to greater insight into Christ and his dealings with the world?

_____

_____

_____

If I were to characterize the circumstances of my life with the metaphor of time, what time is it? Or, if I were to divide my life into chapters, what chapter am I in at the present moment?

_____

_____

_____

What are the issues and circumstances in my life that are a matter of immediacy, even of urgency?

_____

_____

_____

What have been those moments in my life that were pregnant with possibility or meaning? What have been the moments that were the most ripe?

_____

_____

_____

When have I spent time in fruitful reflection? What have been the results?

_____

_____

_____

What parts of my life would be helped if I were to spend significant time in reflection?

_____

_____

_____

What would it mean for me to recognize and honor God's sovereignty? What might it look like when my own will and desires come into contact with God's?

_____

_____

_____

Chapter 3
learning to see

He took the blind man by the hand and led him out of
the village.   —Mark 8:23 (NRSV)

*Prophecy is a matter of seeing near things with their
extensions of meaning and thus of seeing far things close
up. The prophet is a realist of distances, and it is this
kind of realism that you find in the best modern instances
of the grotesque.*   —Flannery O'Connor,
"The Grotesque in Southern Fiction"

I have always been impressed with my father's ability to see. Following
World War II, Dad went to college, after which he became a deputy
with the San Diego County Sheriff's Office. He stayed there throughout
his entire career.

Law enforcement officers are hyper-vigilant. They pay constant attention. They are always watching what's happening right in front of them.
I have never ceased to be amazed at the things Dad actually observes,
especially when I compare his skill with my own grossly underdeveloped
powers of observation. For better, for worse, I am much more comfortable
with my head in a book than I am in the world in which Dad functions. I
will still be learning to see when I lie on my deathbed.

I was attending a writer's workshop in Taos, New Mexico, which
Paula D'Arcy and Roy Carlisle led. Paula gave us a writing assignment.
It included a sentence: *I will die in Paris on a rainy day.* Our instructions
were to take that sentence and to write something about it. When she

assigned us the sentence about dying in Paris, I wondered if Paula had any idea that Nancy and I were scheduled to go to Paris six weeks following our workshop.

After Paula gave her instructions, it was Roy's turn. He was talking about the importance of a writer's paying attention to the things in the real world. Roy knows that I'm not very good at this. I live far more on the interior than I do on the exterior. And when I am pondering, I am lost in the world of my imagination. One of the consequences of this for others is that I become inaccessible to them. I will oftentimes seem aloof. I don't mean to be. But I am comfortable when alone in the world of ideas.

Roy's assignment to me was to pay attention—*with my senses*. I usually take Paula and Roy seriously. And when both of them encourage me to do something, I have my marching orders. After lunch, I decided to go for a walk. And I resolved to do so with *both eyes wide open*. I knew this would be a challenge. I will never forget the time I was walking across the campus, when I was in seminary, with my head in a book. Yes, I read while I walked. I not only walked right into a pillar, I hit it with my head, which I cut, causing me to bleed over myself and the book. That is one of the reasons I knew that Roy's challenge was for me.

So I went for an afternoon walk in Kit Carson Park. As I walked, I happened upon a graveyard. The sign in front of the graveyard read Kit Carson Park Memorial Cemetery. The sign also informed me that the people buried there included several *notables*. All kinds of things came to mind from our morning session with Paula and Roy. I remembered Leslie Weatherhead, a twentieth century English minister, who found a line in a novel that talked about two men passing their time by *admiring the tombs*. Weatherhead thought this to be one of the funniest lines he had ever read. "Imagine admiring the tombs," he used to say. I also remembered one of the participants in our conference, my roommate Hal, asking Roy about the advisability of our writing our own obituaries.

These things in mind, I thought, *Okay, Blackwell. You and Nancy are going to Paris. Paula has given you this assignment, which provokes the idea of dying in Paris on a rainy day. Suppose that it is raining when you go to Paris. Suppose that you die, right then and there. What would it mean for you to have lived a life that is notable?*

That question in mind, I took a deep breath, and I entered the cemetery. And as I admired the tombs, I thought, *You know, Blackwell, so much of the life you've lived isn't all that notable. So much of your life, you haven't lived in the present moment. And most of the time, instead of living, you have played roles. Moreover, it is highly doubtful that any of your performances will ever be nominated for an Oscar.* Now, these thoughts were not morbid. I wasn't paralyzed by dread or despair. I simply realized that I had been present rarely. I had played a lot of roles. And I was far less than happy with many of my performances. But I had rarely been merely me.

So I asked God, right there in the graveyard, *who am I? Who am I without my roles? If you take away the roles of pastor and preacher and teacher and writer, who am I? If you take away the neuroses and the people pleasing and the desire for recognition and acceptance, who am I? And if I were to lose all that, if I were somehow to succeed in living in paradox—losing my life, whether or not it rains when I am in Paris—simply to be right here, right now, with God, as God truly is, what would that mean?*

And then I saw it. I had rounded the corner of the cemetery and was on the home stretch. And to my left was a simple grave marker:

> Rev. F. F. Thomas
> born Mar 4, 1855
> died July 4, 1921
> a friend to mankind

This is the answer I had been looking for. Here was an epitaph meriting aspiration. That gravestone split the veil in two. The fog lifted. My head cleared. *A friend of mankind:* that was how they remembered Rev. F. F. Thomas.

When I returned to my room, I wrote about admiring the tombs, ending with these words: *My greatest desire? It's to offer kindness. It's to see in each person not a role, a title, or a position. It is to see a person—a fellow human being. It is to honor that person with simple, clear kindness. It is not something that I have been particularly skilled or adept at in the past. But by my reckoning, I have 53 days before Nancy and I go to Paris.*

Mark knows that learning to see takes time, and time isn't something he wants to waste. Learning to see involves a long, at times arduous, journey. Mark is eager to get us started. He teaches us to swim by throwing us into the pool. No one can do the work for us, but he's there to help. Just as Paula and Roy served as our mentors during the writing workshop, so has Mark served as mentor and guide for some two thousand years. Mark teaches us to see by offering his insights. These insights, when recognized, reflected on, and implemented, bear the capacity to transform us and bring us to fulfillment—both as individuals and as a community. Though anything but easy, the rewards are beyond calculation.

I find Mark's breadth of vision and depth of insight to be staggering. When Peter Francis, Warden of St. Deiniol's Library, and I were discussing the Gospel of Mark, he remarked, "This is my favorite Gospel." In many respects, it's mine as well. The capacity for insight that Mark renders still astounds me. A part of the reason has to do with Mark's density of discourse—the sheer volume of meaning that Mark packs into the shortest of the Gospels. Fortunately, like any great teacher, Mark doesn't force-feed us. He recognizes that learning to see is an acquired art. It takes time. He does prepare us, but the learning curve is steep. He wants us to learn to see rapidly, and he demands that we *pay attention!* The rewards are mind-boggling. At least, I find it to be so.

Mark's lessons in insight begin, well, at the beginning. He starts off with an echo from the past. This echo is from the beginning of the end of the exile of the people of Judah. In the years 587–586 B.C., the Jews were taken into captivity in Babylon. Thankfully, in the year 539 B.C., through the prophet Isaiah, God announced the beginning of the end of their exile. Mark's Gospel begins with the echo of this announcement:

A voice cries out:
"In the wilderness prepare the way of the Lord,
make straight in the desert a highway for our God."

Mark links the heavenly voice of Isaiah 40 (which says, "In the wilderness prepare the way") with the voice of John the Baptist (which is now in the wilderness crying out, "Prepare the way of the Lord, make his paths *straight*").

The Greek word that Mark uses for "straight" (an adjective) reminds us of his word "immediately" (an adverb) in the Greek language. In other words, the word *straight* is related both to *time* and to *place*. The desert is the place where the crooked will be made straight. For Mark, this refers both to the straightening out of the crooked places as well as straightening out crooked people! Notice also that just as the word *immediately* is a *time* word, it is also a *place* word. We can speak both of doing something immediately (*right now!*) as well as in the immediate vicinity (*right here!*). In other words, *immediately* can mean both *right here* and *right now*. We might say that the word *immediately* embodies a space-time continuum.

What happens next is nothing short of remarkable. As soon as we hear this echo from the past, the future breaks into the present as well. This happens at Jesus's baptism. The story is both simple and straightforward. Jesus comes to the Jordan to present himself to John for baptism. John submerges Jesus into the water. Jesus then rises up out of the water. When he does so, the heavens split open, the spirit descends on Jesus like a dove, and the voice of God speaks directly to Jesus, addressing him, and him alone: "You are my Son, the Beloved; with you I am well pleased."

This story of the baptism of Jesus is the first of several apocalyptic moments in the Gospel of Mark. What do I mean by the word *apocalyptic*? Apocalyptic language portrays the future breaking into the present, charging the entire atmosphere. The future, with all of its opportunities and possibilities, becomes fully present. We ignore its presence at our peril. The time is ripe.

With apocalyptic imagery, it is the *threshold* of heaven that splits open. We do not see into heaven directly, or completely. But we see the atmosphere shot through with shafts of transcendent light. We hear future words spoken right now. We foretaste the heavenly banquet. A European cathedral helps us to imagine an apocalyptic vision. When you enter the cathedral, the presence of heaven is located architecturally on the *inside* of the cathedral. But as you approach the cathedral, you will see the apocalyptic imagery on the cathedral's outside surface—the gargoyles. They do not belong inside of heaven. But they do bear unmistakable divine qualities, and they are under heaven's influence and command. They have the wings of angels, but at the same time they are clearly bestial. Gargoyles express the artistic quality of apocalyptic ambiguity. They evoke wonder and astonishment combined with awe and terror. They warn us: we enter at our own risk. They welcome the past even as they drive us into a future that is ever present in that astonishing place, which is ripe with holiness. There, in heaven on earth, if our eyes and ears are open, future and past launch us to the fulfillment of our present calling.

The inside of the cathedral, in other words, also embodies *kairós*. God's past and future are sustained and present in that place. And God's past and future break into ordinary time as believers answer their call to follow Christ out of the cathedral and into the world, to assist him in his ministry with others.

I find this incredibly brief story of Jesus's baptism to be remarkable in its density for at least two reasons. The first is that it embodies the entire Gospel. To put it another way, the story of the baptism of Jesus presents the Gospel in miniature. Just as Jesus descends into the dark, chaotic waters of baptism, so will he descend into the abyss of crucifixion and death. And just as the heavens split open and the Spirit descends on Jesus like a dove, so will God, so to speak, split the heavens open, reach down, and raise his Son from the dead. The story is brief, but enough of it is there to give us the eyes to see. In the story of the baptism, Mark prepares us to see that when Jesus is crucified and raised, this fulfills his baptism. To put it another way, Jesus's baptism embodies his future death and resurrection. To put it still another way, not only is Jesus's baptism an apocalyptic event, but the baptism prepares us to recognize that the crucifixion and resurrection are the quintessential, defining apocalyptic events as well.

As Mark begins his Gospel, this is one of the most important things that Mark wants us to see. The story of the baptism helps us to recognize what follows. The baptism of Jesus gives us the eyes to see the presence of other future apocalyptic moments as well. The apocalyptic imagery in the baptism of Jesus gives us eyes to recognize the way in which the future is present and the time ripe.

I think that this idea first came to me when reflecting on the second chapter of the Gospel of Mark, the story of the Healing of the Paralytic. Jesus has returned to his home in Capernaum. His popularity has grown so rapidly that a great crowd has filled his house. People are intent on listening to him. They hang on his every word—so much so that they are for the most part oblivious to their surroundings. Four men come to Jesus's home carrying a paralytic on his bed. Their intent is to bring the paralytic to Jesus. However, because of the crowd's total absorption in Jesus, the four men don't receive any help or cooperation from the crowd. This is standing-room only, and no one budges.

Not to worry. These four faithful followers are undaunted. They are also ingenious and unstoppable. What they do is to climb onto the top of Jesus's house and split open the roof. They then carry the paralytic up onto the roof and lower him into the house, laying him right at the feet of Jesus. Jesus takes full note of the faith of the four men: They are willing to do whatever it takes—including taking the roof off Jesus's house—to get a paralytic at Jesus's feet.

Seeing *their* faith (the faith of the four men), Jesus then speaks to the paralytic. I would *expect* Jesus to say to the paralytic, "Rise, take up your bed, and go home." I would expect this, of course, because the man is paralyzed and in need of healing. But what Jesus *actually* says is, "Your sins are forgiven."

Here is where the atmosphere begins to intensify. There were scribes present in Jesus's home, and for some of them, what Jesus said to the man is unthinkable. Jesus has offered the forgiveness of sins. He has done so directly and on his own authority. This was not only presumptuous audacity on Jesus's part, but it also amounted to sheer blasphemy. The way people were *supposed* to get their sins forgiven was to go to the temple in Jerusalem and offer sacrifice. Here, Jesus himself has acted in place of the temple, and he has done so in his own home! This is why the scribes accused Jesus of blasphemy—a most serious charge. Blasphemy is a capital crime, punishable by stoning.

This is where Jesus turns the tables on his adversaries. The scribes held a particular cultural belief. Jesus didn't challenge the belief, but he was completely aware of it. The scribes believed that people couldn't be healed of sickness unless they had first received the forgiveness of sins. So to demonstrate his authority on earth to forgive sins, he did so on their terms—within the framework of their own belief system. Having forgiven the paralytic, he then said, "Rise, take up your bed, and go home." The paralytic obeyed.

The result was not only forgiveness and healing for the paralytic, but Jesus also established his authority in dramatic fashion. In fact, the entire drama is apocalyptic, and we can see this because Mark has shown us how to recognize the apocalyptic drama in the story of Jesus's baptism. Notice the similarities: Just as the heavens split open when Jesus is baptized, so does the roof of Jesus's house split open. And just as the spirit descends on Jesus at his baptism, so now does the paralytic descend to Jesus. And just as God speaks to Jesus at his baptism and says, "You are my son," so now does Jesus say to the paralytic, "Your sins are forgiven," and finally, "Rise, take up your bed and go home." *Mark is showing us that the heavens split open and the future sovereignty of God is present in Jesus's forgiveness of sins. And just as Jesus rises up out of the water when he is baptized, so does the paralytic finally take up his bed and walk.* The kingdom of God is immediately present in Jesus's forgiveness and healing of the paralytic.

Without the story of the baptism of Jesus in Mark 1, we wouldn't be able to see, to recognize, the fulfillment of the presence and power of God in Mark 2. Or, to state it positively, because Mark teaches us how to see in the first chapter, we are ready when things begin to unfold right before our eyes. Mark wants us to be able to recognize the presence of God right where we are. He wants us to see the full glory and significance of the present moment in our immediate environment.

This is what Paula and Roy were trying to teach me when they wanted me always to keep my attention on what is right before me. This is where we will see the heavens split open. Better, this is where we will see that the heavens are split open. It won't typically be in some anticipated dramatic event. It will most often be in ordinary situations lived with extraordinary willingness—right before our eyes.

The heavens were split open in that cemetery on that day in New Mexico. Light from the future was fully present. What was different was that in that particular moment, I was willing to give it recognition. One of the things that I recognized was the truth that I—this body—will one day die. It may even happen in Paris on a rainy day. But whether or not it will be in Paris, my death was fully present, and I was allowing that future to fill me. At the same time, the grave marker recalled a time of stunning significance into my consciousness, where it met my future. It was a time when an ordinary man, the Reverend F. F. Thomas, lived an extraordinary life—with great love. The presence of that love conceived great promise and hope in a moment to which I was for once fully present.

These are matters that Mark's Gospel helps us to recognize with great clarity. God's future and past are fully present. They are right here, right now. The heavens are split open. We need merely to watch and listen!

For Reflection

What might it mean for me to spend some time away from my everyday circumstances to take a fresh look at life?

_____

_____

_____

What might it mean for me to be a little more vigilant in my present circumstances?

_____

_____

_____

Are there things that I keep doing—over and over—that are producing undesirable results?

_____

_____

_____

What kinds of things would I like to happen in my life?

_____

_____

_____

How do I want to be remembered?

_____

_____

_____

What am I willing to do—to take responsibility for—in order to collaborate with God and move towards greater fulfillment?

_____

_____

_____

As I look over my life, when have I seen the heavens split open? How did I respond? How might I respond differently?

_____

_____

_____

Where can I identify the presence of God in my life—right here, right now?

_____

_____

_____

Chapter 4
the deep

And his need, of course, is to be lifted up. There is some-thing in us, as storytellers and as listeners to stories, that demands the redemptive act, that demands that what falls at least be offered the chance to be restored.

—Flannery O'Connor,
"The Grotesque in Southern Fiction"

Teacher, do you not care that we are perishing?
—Jesus's disciples, in Mark 4:38 (NRSV)

Every Monday morning, we went water-skiing. We left the church parking lot at 5:30 a.m. Most of the people were teenagers in our youth group. It was summer in Phoenix. That meant sleeping in. The young people hated getting up early in the morning, but their love of waterski-ing weighed more than their love of sleeping in.

The lake was a half hour from our church. The wind rarely blew at that hour. The water was smooth as glass. The conditions were perfect for waterskiing. And because there were usually only a couple of other boats on the lake, the skiing was not only enjoyable but as safe as we could make it.

When I remember those times on the water, two episodes stand out. One morning, I was sitting on a lawn chair on the lakeshore. In front of me, several of the youth were keeping cool by wading in the water (the Phoenix temperature was 110 degrees). I was watching the lake through my binoculars as my secretary, Pat, drove the boat that pulled one of the skiers (I had taught her how to drive the boat, and by the end of that first summer, she was a pro).

Suddenly, I burst into laughter.

"What's so funny?" someone asked me.

I replied, "Jim just fell, and Wes and Pat haven't noticed. They're just talking away." The reason this struck all us as so funny was that there weren't any other boats nearby, so Jim was in no danger of being hit.

After Pat drove the boat another hundred yards, I could see Pat and Wes realize that they had lost their skier (he was, of course, wearing a life vest). When the boat returned to shore, there was lots of friendly teasing of the two who were in the boat. We all had a good laugh, mainly because all of us were pretty good about laughing at ourselves. At the same time, we were also aware of the danger that the lake posed, especially if it became crowded. We knew that deep water is something to be respected. All of us were happy that there were no mishaps or accidents while we were skiing.

There was another event that same summer that brought no smiles to our faces. Several of us were again sitting on the lakeshore. Suddenly, we heard Danelle screaming at us to get out of the way. We all turned and instantly obeyed. A sport utility vehicle, without a driver, was headed downhill, right for the lake, and we were in its path. We all hastened to get out of the way. As we did so, the vehicle passed right by us and went straight into the lake. By the time it came to a standstill, the top of the car was about four feet under water. What had happened was awful: One of the young men in the group had forgotten to set the parking brake on the family car. He was utterly helpless as he watched it sink into the lake, with bubbles seeming to rise to the surface interminably.

I knew that it was my responsibility to telephone the boy's parents to let them know what had happened. I was not looking forward to talking to the boy's father, but this was nothing compared to what the boy himself was anticipating. We called a tow truck, and we managed to pull the vehicle out of the water (the boy whose car was under water swam down and attached the wench). Thankfully, everyone was safe; but for that day, the fun was over.

What did these two episodes have in common for the people in our youth group? Both brought to the surface of our awareness the threat that lurked under water. For us, the danger was both clear and present. There have been many accidents on the lake where we water-skied. Tragically, once in a while, an accident would prove fatal.

Danger, of course, is not the only thing we associate with water. Water is one of the world's most precious elements. Without water, we die. Although water can be dangerous, it is also refreshing, cleansing, and life-giving. Risks notwithstanding, water is essential. Its functions and qualities are many. Consider the following statements:

May I have a glass of water?
Would you like to go for a swim?
Have you taken your bath?
I was so thirsty!
Our neighbor just put in a new pool. The pool doesn't have a fence around it.
    And there are children in the neighborhood.
Mom, may I go to the beach with my friends?
Dad, let's go river-rafting.
Grandpa, look! I can see my reflection in the water!
I wish it would rain. I am so afraid of losing the harvest.

Each of these statements evokes a different experience of water. One statement can almost take our breath away—the neighbor's pool not having a fence around it, for example. Another might cause our eyes to well up with tears—the grandfather who hears his granddaughter as she discovers that she can see her reflection in the water. Yet another evokes the anticipation of a thrill—the invitation to go river-rafting. Water can create a wealth of experiences.

In Mark's Gospel, the entire story *begins* in water. John the Baptist is in a wilderness, through which the Jordan River runs. There, he is proclaiming a baptism of repentance for the forgiveness of sins. All the people of Jerusalem and Judea go out to the water, confess their sins, and receive the waters of baptism. Jesus himself goes for baptism. In response to Jesus, John says, "I have baptized you with water; but he will baptize you with the Holy Spirit."

This isn't the only time that Mark draws our attention to water. When Jesus calls his first disciples, he does so at the *Sea* of Galilee, where four men are fishing. Before telling and interpreting the Parable of the Sower, Jesus gets into a boat on the *Sea*. From the boat, he addresses the crowd. At the end of his teaching in parables, Jesus is again on the *Sea* of Galilee, this time with his disciples. This is the episode where Jesus calms the storm. In the next episode, Jesus performs an exorcism, which involves delivering a man from a legion of demons by giving them leave to possess a herd of pigs, which jump off a cliff into the *Sea* and are drowned. After feeding the five thousand, Jesus walks on the *water* to his terrified disciples who are facing another storm. After feeding the four thousand, Jesus gets into a boat on the *Sea* with his disciples and attempts, without much success, to help them to understand the meaning of the feeding of the multitudes. When Jesus completes his fourth and final exorcism, we learn that the demon has convulsed the boy, casting him in both fire and *water*. And when teaching his disciples about the fig tree that he has cursed, Jesus tells them, "Have faith in God. Truly, I tell you, if you say to this mountain, 'Be taken up and thrown into the *sea*,' and if you do not doubt in your heart, but believe that what you say will come to pass, it will be done for you." Finally, when the scribes ask Jesus about his authority, he refers back to the *water* of the baptism of John: "Was it from heaven, or of human origin?" Mark focuses on water with remarkable frequency.

Why does Mark feature the element of water with such remarkable frequency? The elements of earth, air, and fire are also in this Gospel, but for Mark, the element of water was essential to what he wanted to convey. What is it about this particular element that Mark finds so vital for fulfilling his purpose in writing? To put it another way, what can water accomplish in the imagination of the reader that the other elements cannot? Unlike earth, fire, and air, water alone is deep, dark, and ominous: "In the beginning, when God created the heavens and the earth, darkness was over the face of the deep waters." Water embodies the primordial chaos and the absence of life prior to creation. It is difficult to fathom anything more terrifying than to be submerged and trapped in a lifeless abyss. With water come floods, tempests, storms, drowning, and devastation. The danger that water poses is finally beyond our power to control absolutely. One has only to observe the aftermath of Hurricane Katrina to know of water's capacity to cause despair.

Water is the element that is best suited to Mark's insight: The Good News is that in Jesus Christ, the time is ripe for God to deliver us from the dark, chaotic abyss in which we are drowning. In Jesus Christ, the power of God is present to deliver us from whatever abyss threatens to swallow us up. Jesus Christ is immediately present with us—right here, right now—when we are drowning in a sea of despair. The Good News is that Jesus Christ actively seeks to deliver us from the abyss, placing us on solid ground.

Mark's insight also brings us to the heart of what it means to follow this Messiah. In the first chapter of Mark, the second time that Mark features water (the first is at Jesus's baptism) is at the Sea of Galilee. Jesus passed along the shore. He saw two fishermen, Simon Peter and Andrew, casting their nets into the sea. Jesus called to them, saying, "Follow me, and I will make you fish for people!" Simon and Andrew left their nets immediately and followed Jesus. A little farther along the shore, they encountered James and John, the Sons of Zebedee. In the same spirit, Jesus called them as well. James and John left everything and followed Jesus.

Just as the story of the Baptism of Jesus teaches us to see, so does the story of the Call of the First Four Disciples. With this remarkably simple story, Mark renders a picture of discipleship. Following Christ is both similar to fishing and also different. Whereas fishing involves casting nets into the water to catch fish for the purpose of consuming them, *following Jesus involves assisting him in casting the net into the sea, rescuing people from whatever abyss that is consuming them and placing them on solid ground.* Mark's insight is that *in Christ, the time has arrived for our deliverance from the terrors that engulf us, and we are called to assist Christ as he seeks to deliver others.* That's what it means to be a disciple of Christ.

The first large section of Mark's Gospel (1:1—8:21) involves learning to recognize the presence of the power of God to deliver the world from The Deep. At the heart of this first section are three critical stories, with which Mark conveys his stunning vision. The first involves the Calming of the Sea (we will address the other two later in this book). As with the stories of Jesus's Baptism and the Calling of the Disciples, this story's simplicity is matched by its astonishing insight into the nature of the Good News.

The story comes at the end of the fourth chapter. Having finished teaching and interpreting parables, Jesus said to his disciples, "Let us cross to the other side of the sea." Leaving the crowd behind them, Jesus's followers took him into the boat and set sail. Mark adds a curious line to his narration:

They took Jesus *as he was*. Well, just how was Jesus, anyway? The answer is simple: Jesus was asleep. This wasn't the last time that Jesus would be tired and drained from his work with the crowd. In the sixth chapter, Jesus said to his disciples, "Come away to a deserted place all by yourselves and rest a while." The disciples found following Jesus to be demanding work. Jesus and his disciples frequently felt drained. This seems to be why Jesus was in the back of the boat, sleeping.

It is worth noting that like the stories of the Baptism of Jesus and the Call of the Disciples, this story also prefigures what will follow. Just as Jesus is asleep in the boat on the sea, so will he be laid in the tomb, following his death by crucifixion. And just as the disciples rouse Jesus from his sleep, so will God raise him from the dead. For as the disciples made their journey, a great windstorm arose on the sea. Waves beat into the boat, which was almost completely swamped with water. In a panic, the disciples went to the back of the boat and woke Jesus: "Teacher, do you not care that we are perishing?"

When Jesus woke, he addressed the storm. Jesus rebuked the wind, and commanded the sea to be still: "Peace! Be calm."

What followed was a tranquility that left the disciples astounded. Jesus chastised them: "Why are you afraid? Have you still no faith?" They disciples are dumbfounded: "Who then is this, that even the wind and the sea obey him?"

I still find this story to be astonishing. Its effect is to convey to our imaginations the power of Christ to deliver us from the terror of the abyss. This story gives us insight into the nature of Christ's dealings with us as well as the possibilities for our implementing (living) this vision in the world.

This reality of the depth of the power of God struck me so forcefully that I wanted to find a way to convey it to people I served in the church and at the retreats where I spoke. I wanted people to experience and understand something about what the power to calm the seas and tempests in our day looked like. As a part of my reflection, I will sometimes compose stories that I hope will reflect some aspect of the deep truth that a biblical writer conveys. Here is one that I composed as a part of my response to the Gospel of Mark:

At the age of fourteen, Sara had never known an occasion when her father had hugged her, complimented her, or told her that he was proud of her. She finally gave up hope that this would happen. But this did not completely quench her enthusiasm for life.

One day, as she arrived home from school, Sara burst through the door. "Mom! Dad! They're having a play at school. I auditioned for one of the parts, and . . ."

"Shut up, wench! We couldn't care less about your stupid play."

That was the moment when Sara decided never again to share with her parents something that was precious to her. Their rejection was so painful that, in an effort to anesthetize her pain, Sara began drinking. Before too many months, her friends were offering her marijuana. She didn't refuse. In this way, Sara steadily became more and more numb.

Life continued in this way for two years, till one day, when she arrived home from school, she encountered a sight that horrified her. In the kitchen, sitting on the floor, with her legs spread apart, with a half-empty bottle of bourbon between her legs and her back against the cupboard, was her mother. Her chin was down to the bottom of her neck, and she was clearly drunk. Sara asked, "Mom, what on earth happened?"

Her mother's voice sounded lifeless. "Your father's left, and he isn't coming back."

For the first time in years, Sara actually felt compassion for her mother. Involuntarily, she responded: "Oh, Mom, is there anything I can do to help?"

Sara could barely take in what happened next. She saw her mother's chin begin to rise, and she could then see her mother's expression. It had a look of wicked contempt and hatred. Her mother glared at Sara. She mocked Sara with sardonic laughter: "Is there anything I can do to help? Is there anything I can do to help? You want to help? Get out of my life! I never want to see your face again!"

Sara was reeling. She wanted out of there, so she left. She didn't know where she was going, and she didn't care. She just wanted to get as far away from her mother as she could.

What she did was to make her way to the Greyhound Bus Depot. There, she bought a ticket to its terminal destination and got on board.

When the bus arrived at its final destination, it pulled into a large depot, with long slanting, parallel lines. The bus driver pulled the vehicle between two of them near the end.

At the other end of the depot was a hot pink and purple Cadillac, with gold trim and white sidewall tires. Standing next to the car was a man with gold rings on most of his fingers, three gold necklaces, and diamond-studded teeth. The man scrutinized every person who disembarked from the bus. When he saw Sara, he knew that she was the one he wanted.

The man walked straight to Sara and questioned her boldly. "Hi, Baby Doll. Got any place to go?"

Sara was so startled by his directness and air of confidence that her response was both truthful and involuntary: "No, I don't."

"Come on, then. I'll take care of you."

For the next two weeks, he put Sara through her initiation, at the conclusion of which she found herself working the streets of the city she had escaped to.

39
THE DEEP

In the process, Sara had developed such a self-loathing that not even the hard drugs that her master gave her could numb her pain. Sara became so self-destructive that she finally resolved to end it all.

It was her day off—Sunday. Sara's plan was to take the bus to the bridge that crossed the harbor of this port city. From the middle of the bridge, Sara would jump off.

On her way to the bus stop, Sara happened to walk past a downtown church, the entrance of which went all the way to the sidewalk. Almost involuntarily, she veered towards the entrance of the church. She found herself attracted by a sound she had never heard. It was the sound of a pipe organ.

At the entrance to the church stood a man who had served as an usher of that church almost as long as anyone could remember. He loved his job so much, and he was so skilled that before Sara realized what was happening, she found herself in the back pew of this downtown church, with a bulletin in her hand, at the opening of the first worship service she had ever attended.

With the congregation, she stood as they sang the opening hymn. This was followed by an affirmation of faith, a prayer of confession, and a baptism. The baptism intrigued Sara. She had never seen anything like it.

Half way through the service, the pastor started to preach. His text was from the end of the fourth chapter of the Gospel of Mark—the story of Jesus calming the storm. He told the congregation how "the disciples were in the boat with Jesus. Suddenly, a fierce wind swept down upon them. The sea became more and more choppy. The boat began to bob up and down. Before long, the disciples were in the thick of a violent storm. The wind was whipping them in the face, waves were sloshing over the boat, and they were afraid that they were going to sink and drown.

"The disciples began to panic. The storm was overwhelming them. In their fear, they began yelling at each other: 'Where's Jesus?'

"'I don't know!'

"'What do you mean, you don't know?'

"'I can't mind everything!'

"Another disciple yelled, 'I know where he is!'

"'Where?'

"'He's in the back of the boat, asleep!'

"'Asleep?'

"And then, one of them rushed to the back of the boat, grabbed Jesus, shook him, and yelled, 'Master, wake up! We're gonna die! Don't you care?'

"And Jesus, roused from his sleep, looked at his disciples, and then commanded the wind and the sea, 'Be calm. Be still. Peace.'

"And the winds subsided. And the sea became still. And there was a great calm."

The pastor paused, and then he spoke these words. Sara felt as though he was speaking to her alone.

"There is someone here in whom a great storm is raging in your life. The storm is fierce and overwhelming. You feel confused, blinded, and out of control. You have been debilitated. You sense no hope, and you wonder if there will ever be another day.

"Jesus has a word, and he speaks it to you: 'I have come to calm the storm that is raging in your life. I have come to calm your storm.

I have come to soothe you. I have come to bring you comfort and peace. I have come to tell you I love you. There is no person on earth whom I love more than you. I am here, right now, with you. I am holding you. I am offering you comfort. You have hope. I am your hope. I will never leave you. I am with you always. Be still. Be calm. I am filling you with peace.'"

At the end of the worship service, Sara felt a firm, but gentle hand take her arm. It was the usher, who had drawn her into the sanctuary. He said to her, "Come with me."

The usher took Sara to the pastor's study. "Stay right here. Don't go away. I'll be right back." The usher then went to the pastor, who was greeting his flock. He took the pastor by the arm and said, "There'll be no coffee hour for you today, Buddy." He directed the pastor to go to his study.

When Sara saw the man who spoke to her the words of Jesus for the first time, she fell at his feet, poured out her story, and cried like a baby.

After she told her story, both of them were silent. The pastor reflected that there are times in our lives when we are called to do something of immeasurable importance for someone else's benefit. He knew this was one such occasion. He also had the humility to realize that he could not help Sara by himself. The pastor said to Sara, "Wait right here. I promise I'll be back."

He left his office to go to the fellowship hall. Fortunately, this was a congregation that spent lots of time at coffee hour, visiting. The pastor found the people he needed.

When he returned to his study, the pastor said to Sara, "Come with me." He took her to the church parlor. In the parlor was a circle of twelve chairs, ten of which were occupied by members of the church.

The pastor offered Sara one of the chairs and then sat down beside Sara. He then spoke:

"Sara, these are all members of our congregation. We have a gift we want to offer you: We want to invite you to become a part of our church, and we want to give you a home. We want our church to be your home."

The pastor then introduced a man and a woman to Sara. "They have two grown daughters who no longer live at home. That means that they have two empty bedrooms. They are offering their home to you. You can choose which bedroom you like. Choose both of them, if you want. Nothing is required of you. We simply want you to know that God loves you, you can count on us, and we want to be your family. What do you say?"

Sara could barely comprehend the invitation. Nothing like this had ever happened to her.

"Do you have any questions?" they asked.

Sara thought for a moment, gathering her thoughts. Finally, she replied: "During the church service, you took a baby in your arms and put water on her head."

"Yes," the pastor replied. "I baptized her."

"If I say yes to your offer, will you baptize me?"

That group of twelve got up from the church parlor, went into the sanctuary, and gathered around the baptismal font. All joined hands. Three times, the pastor put water on Sara's head: "Sara, I baptize you in the name of the Father and the Son and the Holy Spirit."

At that moment, those twelve people became the church—right there in the sanctuary.

Mark's great insight involved recognizing that in Christ, God's power to deliver people from the abyss is fully present—right here, right now, before our very eyes. By writing his Gospel, Mark calls upon us to follow Jesus—to assist Christ as he seeks, finds, and delivers people engulfed in The Deep. This involves a fair amount of recognition as we learn to see what is right in front of us, recognizing both our own circumstances and the situations that entrap and paralyze others. This also involves ample time for reflection—sometimes alone, other times in dialogue together—as we seek to understand how Christ calls us to follow him. Finally, and perhaps most important, this involves implementation. If the pastor and congregation in the story had merely verbalized their compassion and sent Sarah on her way, would anything have changed for the better? Would Sarah have enjoyed the opportunity for her own transformation? Would the congregation have answered its call, been transformed, and come to the appropriate place of their own fulfillment? Mark's vision and hope are clear: recognition, reflection, and implementation are all essential to our growth in Christ. We have a part to play. Each of us counts.

For Reflection

What has been my experience of the deep? Where have I know the dark, ominous abyss? When have I felt as though I was sinking?

_____

_____

_____

What kinds of storms have raged in my life? When have I felt hopeless, or out of control?

_____

_____

_____

When did the power of God deliver me from threatening circumstances?

_____

_____

_____

Where is the solid ground in my life? Where am I sufficiently safe that I can breathe and get my bearings?

_____

_____

_____

Who do I know that is "sinking?" What might God be calling me to do to assist Christ in helping that person to solid ground?

_____

_____

_____

In what circumstances can I recognize Christ speaking to me and calming the storm that threatens my life?

_____

_____

_____

What am I willing to do to respond to Christ's power calming my storm? What steps will I take? When will I take them?

_____

_____

_____

Chapter 5 ~ Demons

My name is Legion, for we are many.
　　　　　　　—The Demoniac, in Mark 5:9 (NRSV)

It cannot see man as determined; it cannot see him as totally depraved. It will see him as incomplete in himself, as prone to evil, but as redeemable when his own efforts are assisted by grace. And it will see this grace as working through nature, but as entirely transcending it, so that a door is always open to possibility and the unexpected in the human soul.
　　　　　　　—Flannery O'Connor,
　　"The Catholic Novelist in the Protestant South"

The officer heard screaming. As he approached the front porch, an 18-year-old girl ran from the home, threw her arms around the officer, and shouted, "Don't let them hurt me!" The *Northwest Indiana Times* reported that the girl suffered from a mental disability. She told police that her mother and stepfather had burned her with cigarettes, had administered electrical shock to various parts of her body, raped her with a fireplace poker, forced her to eat cigarettes, and had kept her locked in her room.

My family knows the girl. When she was living in our city, she was in foster care with an extraordinary, devoted family. Along with her family, she had been a guest in our home. When I learned of what happened to the girl, I felt a sensation of being kicked in the stomach. Because I knew her, to learn what happened to her sickened me. It reminded me of times I had had the *wind knocked out of me* when I was a child.

We all had the same sensation when we learned that two young men with firearms had entered Columbine High School and murdered several students and a teacher in cold blood. And of course, we will never forget the morning of September 11, 2001.

Jesus knew what it felt like to have the wind knocked out of him. On several occasions, I have read that when Jesus was crucified, the cause of death was asphyxiation. But long before his crucifixion, Jesus had the same experience of feeling the wind knocked out of him. When Jesus would learn that a person suffered cruelty or intolerable circumstances, his compassion ran so deep that he felt as though he had been kicked in the stomach. The first time that this happened was when Jesus encountered a leper. Mark reports this story at the end of the first chapter. The leper approached Jesus, knelt before him, and begged Jesus to make him clean: "I know you can do this. Are you willing? Would you consider healing me?"

Scholars who translate the Greek into English so that we can understand the Gospels sometimes face difficult challenges. Occasionally, there is no English word that expresses the full range of meaning of a Greek word. Mark says that when the leper bowed ever so respectfully before Jesus and supplicated him, Jesus was moved with *pity*. This is true. Jesus was. The leper's condition broke Jesus's heart. There is also more. The word that Mark uses, *splangchintzomai*, refers to compassion. But it also refers to one's bowels. It conveys a compassion that is so deep that it feels like being kicked in the stomach. It's what we feel when we are betrayed. It's what we feel when learning that someone has been tortured. I am close to someone who lost eighteen friends when the Twin Towers collapsed on September 11, 2001. When she shared that with me, I could see her reliving the sickening feeling of being kicked in the stomach, as she remembered the agonizing horror.

When we remember September 11 or Columbine High School, or when we learn that an innocent girl has been tortured, why do we feel like we've been kicked in the stomach? I think that we feel this way because we are encountering bald-faced evil. For two grown adults to incarcerate a help-less young woman in their home and to torture her with electrical shock is brutal evil. There are other words for it, to be sure. But to refuse or fail to recognize the evil is to turn a blind eye and to miss the mark. The perpetrators of torture were possessed by an abyss of evil, just as the young woman was entrapped in the resulting abyss of torture.

One of the things that Mark accomplished in his Gospel was to give us the eyes to recognize evil—including the evil in ourselves, the evil to which we are all vulnerable. The early stories in Mark's Gospel prepare us to see. The story of the Baptism of Jesus embodies the Gospel in miniature: Just as Jesus descends into the waters of baptism, so will he descend into the abyss of death by torture. And just as Jesus emerges from the water as the heavens split open and the Spirit descends on Jesus like a dove, with the words, "You are my son," so will God reach to the crucified and buried son and raise him from the dead. And just as Jesus calls four fishermen to leave their nets and follow him as he will teach them to fish for people, so will following Christ involve assisting him as he casts his net into the dark abyss to draw people out of the chaos that engulfs them, placing them on the sufficient security of solid ground.

As with these episodes, the story of the exorcism in the synagogue of Capernaum prepares us to recognize another aspect of Christ's ministry—recognizing evil and the power of God to deliver us from it. The story is straightforward. It was the Sabbath that followed the call of the first disciples. Jesus was at his home in Capernaum, which is located northeast of the Sea of Galilee. Jesus entered his home synagogue to teach. Mark doesn't tell us the contents of Jesus's teaching, but he does tell us that the people found Jesus's teaching to be compelling and utterly astounding. Jesus's teaching was authoritative. It rang true.

Because of the authenticity of Jesus's teaching, there was a man in the synagogue who felt threatened: "What have you to do with us, Jesus of Nazareth? Have you come to destroy us?" This man recognizes Jesus: "I know who you are, the Holy One of God."

Why does this man recognize Jesus? He is possessed by evil, and evil recognizes the presence of goodness. Evil also feels the threat of goodness. At least, this particular evil person does.

Jesus's response is to *rebuke* the evil in this man. This is how Jesus handles evil throughout the entire Gospel: "Be silent, and come out of him!"

The result was immediate and straightforward. The evil spirit convulsed the man, and crying with a loud voice, left him. The people in the synagogue were utterly astounded: "What is this? A new teaching—with authority! He commands even unclean spirits, and they obey him." As a consequence, Jesus became instantly famous.

Why didn't Mark share the contents of Jesus's teaching? He is simply showing us that the heart of Jesus's ministry includes recognizing and confronting evil, from which he then delivers us. Much of Jesus's ministry involves casting out demons: "And he went throughout Galilee . . . casting out demons" (Mark 1:39).

Because Mark didn't tell us the contents of Jesus's teaching in the synagogue, and because Mark didn't tell us any more about the man than that he was possessed by a demon, he leaves us curious, wanting to know and to understand more. How do we recognize evil? What does it look like? One of the things that make Mark's Gospel so remarkable is his insight into evil, for what he does is to show us a human soul that is possessed. Better, he shows us Jesus confronting an abyss of evil that engulfs a human soul and delivering that person from the evil with which he is possessed. Not only does the story of the Exorcism in the Synagogue prepare us to recognize evil more fully, so does the story of the Calming of the Sea. In this episode, Jesus delivers the terrifying stormy sea from its violent threat. In the story that immediately follows, Jesus confronts an internal storm of violence that renders the person a threat both to himself and to others.

Having calmed the storm, Jesus, with his disciples, arrives at the eastern shore of the Sea of Galilee. This is the country of the Gerasenes. Here, Jesus is confronted by a man whose insides are riddled with contradictions. This man's soul is at war with itself. One part of his character is in constant conflict with the others. The man is alive, but he lives among the tombs, the place where the dead reside. But unlike the dead, the man is self-destructive and beyond restraint. He howls. He beats and bruises himself with stones. He wrenches apart his chains. When he sees Jesus, he bows and worships the Son of the Most High God and, at the same time, demands that Jesus depart and leave him to his own torment. His greatest terror is the torment that he believes Jesus will cause.

By juxtaposing the story of the demoniac with the Calming of the Sea, Mark draws a link between the stormy sea on the one hand and the storm inside of the demoniac on the other. In this story, not only does Mark give us a picture of the man's soul, but he also opens a window on Jesus's dealings with this inner tempest. As with the Healing of the Blind Man (Mark 8:22–30), this man's healing, or deliverance from evil, isn't instantaneous. Jesus first commands the demons, "Come out of the man, you unclean spirit!" After this, Jesus asks the demon its name. The demon replies, "My name is Legion; for we are many." His name, in other words, expresses the condition of his soul, which is in constant uproar.

Terrified of what Jesus will demand, the demons beg not to be banished from the country. Nearby, a herd of pigs was feeding. "Send us into the swine; let us enter them" (Mark 5:12).

It is worth remembering that Judaism regards pigs as unclean. The demons have begged to possess the symbols of abomination. Jesus grants their request. The demons take leave of the man and enter the swine. The pigs respond by going mad. They rush down a steep bank, jump into the water, and drown in the sea. The dark abyss, in other words, receives the demon-possessed pigs, becoming the instrument of their destruction.

Not surprisingly, the swineherds run to the town to tell others what has happened. This provokes curiosity among the people. They come to the scene, only to discover that the man who had been possessed by the legion of demons is sitting and in his right mind. Jesus has delivered him of the legion of evil that has held the man hostage. Not fully understanding the events, the people are scared.

The next exchange is curious. The people want Jesus to leave. Earlier in the Gospel, when Jesus healed, the people wanted to be with him. Now, they want him out of there. Instead of celebrating Jesus's power to deliver someone from evil, they beg Jesus to leave. As Jesus complies with their request, the man whom Jesus has delivered approaches Jesus and pleads with Jesus to take him in. Jesus flatly refuses: "Go home to your friends, and tell them how much the Lord has done for you, and what mercy he has shown you" (Mark 5:19).

It's hard for me to imagine a more stark portrayal of the inner turmoil of the human soul. To read this story with genuine reflection takes the greatest of humility. Where do we find the grace to do so? I find it helpful to recognize that the best people who have lived have faced the demons within.

This past semester, I was teaching the letters of the apostle Paul. I try to persuade my students to recognize and accept the differences within the New Testament, not because I want to destroy their faith or to tear apart the Bible. My goal, rather, is to help the students to see the unique insights of each author. The problem with an approach that merely seeks the commonalities in the New Testament, the places of agreement, is that we can miss the particular things that each writer bears witness to. Having said that, as the end of the semester approached, I told my students, "I want to show you some important matters that Paul *shares* with other writers—similar ideas that they express in different, complementary ways." I did so by comparing Mark's story of the Gerasene Demoniac with what Paul wrote in Romans 7. In this passage, Paul shows great humility as he opens his heart. He doesn't beat up on himself. He doesn't say, "Woe is me. I am the scum of the earth, the worst person ever to have lived." But neither does he sugar-coat his own struggles. Instead, Paul provides a window of self-disclosure that gives us permission to acknowledge the struggle that we have with inner conflict. Paul writes, "I am . . . sold into slavery under sin. I do not understand my own actions. For I do not do what I want, but I do the very thing I hate. . . . In fact it is no longer I that do it, but sin that dwells within me. For I know that nothing good dwells within me, that is, in my flesh. I can will what is right, but I cannot do it. For I do not do the good I want, but the evil I do not want is what I do. . . . I see in my members another law at war with the law of my mind, making me captive to the law of sin that dwells in my members. Wretched man that I am! Who will rescue me from this body of death?"

Paul's answer is that the power by which God raised Christ from the dead is what will deliver him. Notice what Paul does here. Whereas Mark gives us a picture of the soul of the demoniac, Paul discloses his own struggle with inner contradictions and the sin that evil produces. One of the effects of his doing so is to give us permission to do likewise. There is evil in all of us. As Aleksander Solzhenitsyn discovered, the line that separates good from evil runs not between countries, races, or political parties. It runs right down the human heart. There is good and evil in all of us. Flannery O'Connor put it this way: "Evil is not a problem to be solved [abstractly, or in theory], but a mystery to be endured." She recognized that the source of grace with which we endure the mystery of evil that both Mark and Paul wrote about with such poignancy is Christ.

How, then, do we find the humility necessary to deal with the evil within? One of the things I greatly admire about Flannery O'Connor is that she won't allow her readers to become so obsessed by theory and abstraction that they reduce evil (and people, for that matter) to mere formulas. I mention this because I find it helpful to think of genuine human transformation as unfolding in three complementary phases—recognition, interpretation and reflection, and implementation. In saying this, I do not intend to reduce insights into formulas. I don't think in terms of a *recipe for fulfillment—one size fits all*. I'm not interested in selling snake oil, and I'm not particularly fond of literary parlor tricks.

I do think, however, that our ability to recognize the evil within is greatly strengthened by our willingness to spend time in honest reflection. I also think that the willingness to face up to the evil within can be effective if we approach self-reflection with a willingness to welcome and implement whatever grace God provides for its removal and our fulfillment as human beings. Evil is what stands in the way of our rising to the full stature of our humanity. Becoming fully human is a long, sometimes arduous journey, but what more merits such aspiration?

To assist us in confronting the evil within, between the stories of Jesus's first exorcism and the exorcism of the Gerasene Demoniac, Mark gives us a clear picture of aspects of evil to which we are all vulnerable. What, then, can we know about the nature of the evil that Christ exorcises? How does it provoke us to act? What are its effects?

Evil leads us to banish people and to destroy relationships. In the Gospel of Mark, this takes the form of ostracism. Lepers, for example, were sent into exile. The people of Israel wanted to maintain ritual purity. There is nothing wrong with that. It is an admirable goal. The way some went about it, however, had consequences for lepers, who were in no way at fault.

Evil leads us to object strongly to the forgiveness of sins. This can take the shape of protesting someone else's receiving forgiveness, or perhaps in our own obstinate grudge-carrying. Forgiveness is oftentimes a process. It can take a long time to come to fruition. The alternative is to choose to be possessed by bitterness and wrath that not only destroy relationships, but the very people who are militantly unforgiving.

Evil leads us to refuse hospitality to the stranger, the sinner, or the sick. We can be prone to incarcerate ourselves in prisons of our own devising.

Evil leads us to refuse to celebrate. Not only will we not weep with those who weep, but we will not rejoice with those who rejoice. We'll instead opt for the pity party and feeling sorry for ourselves.

Evil leads us to force our ways of doing things on others, even if our ways don't work. We can be so protective of our own approach to living life and solving problems that effectiveness and goodness cease to be legitimate issues. Instead, it's either *my way, or the highway*.

Evil leads us to care more for pretense and appearance (looking good) than to legitimate human need and justice. We can be prone to concern ourselves far more with what others think or maintaining control and reputation than with seeking resolution in ways that are mutually beneficial and liberating.

Evil leads us to make an idol of traditions to which we cling to the point of rigidity. We can become so obsessed with our own tastes, preferences, and sensibilities that we can act as though they are the absolute standard by which all others are bound to think and operate.

Evil leads us to refuse to oppose other people's being harmed, especially when we consider those harmed to pose a threat to our preferences or rationales for decision-making.

Evil leads us to confuse the difference between good and evil. We become liable to call evil good and good evil. The result is that we become prone to opposing goodness, especially when it conflicts with our own interests, agendas, and rationales.

Finally, evil leads us to live a life that is divided. Not only will we be at war with those around us, we will be at war with our best selves—the self-evident good within.

Where, then, do we begin? How do we cooperate with Christ, whose claim is that the time for our deliverance from the demonic abyss of evil and sin is fully present? When we know of circumstances that the eighteen-year-old young woman faced as she was taken captive and tortured, we can recognize the gravity of the stark forces of evil and the cruelty that is its ultimate fruit. We can then ask Christ to help us to recognize and reflect on what we need to know about the evil within us. Scary? I have found it to be so. I have also found that the fear greatly lessons when I go into my times of reflection with a commitment to cooperate with Christ as he does what I cannot do. The power to deliver is finally his. I am not sure that he ever allows the full weight of the evil of which we are capable to come fully to consciousness. I wonder if we could understand such complete self-knowledge. But I do believe that when we are genuinely willing, Christ brings to consciousness what we need to know. I also believe that he joins us as partners in our reflections. He, too, fully understands that the spirit may be willing, but the flesh is awfully weak. Paul understood this as well. When, however, our commitment to deliverance from evil and sin is genuine, grace follows. It then becomes our delightful responsibility to recognize it, welcome it, and to give grace a home within.

For Reflection

When have I felt as though I had the wind knocked out of me? What were the circumstances?

_____

_____

_____

When has someone else's suffering filled me with compassion? How did I respond? How might I respond in the future?

_____

_____

_____

In what ways am I like, or unlike, the Gerasene Demoniac? Where, for example, am I at war inside myself? What does my inner turmoil look like?

Or, where is my life riddled with contradictions? Where am I a person of conflicting loyalties?

_____

_____

_____

What kind of evil do I face or encounter? How do I know it to be evil? What might Christ be calling me to do to confront and deal with the evil that I face?

_____

_____

_____

Are there ways in which I resist letting go of evil? Are there ways that I try to drive Christ out of my life? What kinds of changes has Christ been trying to make in my life that I have resisted?

_____

_____

_____

Are there places in my life where Christ has been seeking to encounter me? How have I been responding? Have I been welcoming Christ? Driving him away? What am I willing to do differently? How will I treat Christ today—right here and now?

_____

_____

_____

Chapter 6
the crush of the crowd

We were visiting our friends Jennifer, Doug, and Jacob over the holidays. Over dinner, we got to reminiscing. They told us about one particular holiday they had spent at Disneyland. The climax of their time there involved a parade, after which everyone was to leave. The park was closing.

Jennifer told us how there were so many people that she began to feel claustrophobic. She had difficulty not panicking. The crush of people was just overwhelming. They could barely move, and no one could move very far. What they did was simple. They managed to keep their wits about them by moving to a table. The table was nearby, but it took enormous effort to make it even that far.

They made it, and there they sat. They decided that the best thing they could do was simply to sit and wait out the storm, so to speak. It took a long time for the crowd to thin out, but once it did, they could leave the park with much greater calm.

Jesus knew about crowds. Owing to his healing, huge crowds gathered around him. Jesus tried to prevent this, but he tried in vain. When he healed a person, he would admonish that person so say nothing about what he had done. That those whom Jesus had healed had difficulty keeping their mouths shut is understandable—especially when their illness entailed years of suffering. The result for Jesus and his disciples was difficult. People wanted to be close to Jesus. They wanted to see him; they wanted to hear him. Many wanted his healing power for themselves. The outcome was that they mobbed him, and the effect could be suffocating—like drowning in a sea of people.

One of the things that make Mark's Gospel so remarkable has to do with the way in which he brings images together. The story of the Healing of the Gerasene Demoniac immediately follows the Calming of the Storm. The close proximity of these two episodes helps us to recognize that the terrifying chaos that Jesus confronts in the sea is like the terrifying war that is going on inside the man possessed by a legion of demons. Both are aspects of an overwhelming abyss of evil, recrimination, chagrin, and despair.

The crowd is also one of Mark's images of the frightful abyss. In the third chapter of Mark, as Jesus went to the sea, such a great multitude mobbed him that he had to have a boat into which he could escape, so that the crowd would not crush him. Jesus had healed so many people "that all who had diseases pressed upon him to touch him" (Mark 3:10). The next time that Jesus returned to his home in Capernaum, a huge crowd gathered. The crush of people was so great that people couldn't eat. In the fourth chapter of Mark, Jesus taught people by the Sea of Galilee. This time, he used a boat for his pulpit. The crowd had gathered on the land, "beside the sea." Later in the Gospel, Jesus would characterize the crowd as chaotic—like sheep without a shepherd.

Jesus knew how to read a crowd. He also knew that the crowd could be a terrifying abyss, as for a short time it was for our friends Doug and Jennifer. It is true that there are people who want to lose themselves in the crowd, which is to say, they want to stay under the radar and remain anonymous. In Mark's Gospel, however, there are people who have been swallowed by the crowd, just as Jesus's disciples were in danger of being swallowed up by the dark-grey, deep sea.

One of these was the Woman with the Hemorrhage. In the fifth chapter, Jesus and his disciples returned by boat from the land of the Gerasenes. As he came to the lakeshore, once again a large crowd gathered around him. One of those in the crowd was a public figure—Jairus, the ruler of the synagogue. Jairus sought Jesus because his twelve-year-old daughter was sick to the point of death. The man begged Jesus to come to his home. Jesus agreed, making his way.

Throughout this journey, a large crowd practically smothered Jesus. In this crowd was a woman who had been hemorrhaging. For twelve years, she had suffered pain, bleeding, ostracism, disgrace, and degradation: the fifteenth chapter of Leviticus says that a woman who is hemorrhaging is unclean. Being unclean, she is allowed contact with no one. Any person she touched would become unclean. Any object she touched would be unclean as well. The last place she would be allowed would be near the temple in Jerusalem—the place where the people received the forgiveness of sins and enjoyed hospitality with God. Because of her illness, this woman was kept in exile: in captivity to uncleanness, she was banished from the family of God.

As if suffering and ostracism weren't bad enough, the woman had also visited several physicians. Tragically, she had received nothing from them that would help. Under their "care," she lost all of her money, and her condition worsened.

She had, however, heard about Jesus. She had heard things he had said, stories he had told. She had also heard that he had healed. Finding herself in the crowd that was pressing upon Jesus, the woman thought to herself, *if I could just touch him. I don't need to speak with him. I don't need his attention. But I know that he has the power to make me well. If I could just touch his clothing . . . .*

In her agony, in her desperation, from the depths of her suffering, the woman worked her way through the crowd, reached out, and just got a hold on Jesus's clothing. The effect was immediate. No sooner had she touched his garment than immediately the hemorrhaging stopped. She felt—deep in her body—the freedom, the relief. She had been healed of her disease. The power of Christ had delivered her from the constant bleeding. She knew she was well.

Sensing that power had flowed from him, Jesus immediately turned on the crowd and demanded, "Who touched me? Who touched my clothing?"

The disciples were the first to respond: *What do you mean, who touched you? Everyone is touching you. Look at this crowd. It's a mob. Everyone is thronging about you. Come on! Let's get to the home of the ruler of the synagogue!*

Jesus, however, will have none of their impatience or self-importance. Instead, he studied the crowd. He wanted to know who had done it. He also wanted to know why.

His eyes naturally finally settled on the woman. She was the obvious one. She knew what she had done. She had reached out, touched Jesus, taken his healing power without first asking permission, and in the process made Jesus unclean as well. After all, she was unclean, and anyone she touched became unclean as well. And now she had been caught. It wouldn't have been difficult for Jesus to know that she was the one.

So the woman approached Jesus, fell at his feet, and told him the whole truth. And what is the whole truth? It was the years of sickness. It was the years of suffering. It was the years of pain. It was the hope that was all but extinguished. It was the humiliation of being ostracized. It was the shame of knowing that any person you touched became unclean. It was the disgrace of being a permanent outsider. It was the desperation of being alone in her illness.

And then, how she had heard about Jesus—the words, the stories, the healing. She had heard that he had touched others. Finally, she told Jesus about being lost in this crowd, working her way forward, not wanting to bother Jesus, not wanting to inconvenience him. But she did touch him. She took his healing power. She had neglected first to ask for it. And so doing, she had made Jesus unclean—she had made him bear her sickness in himself.

By custom, Jesus has the right to be furious with the woman. Anger, however, is the furthest thing from his imagination. When Jesus speaks, he addresses the woman as a member of his family. He calls her daughter: "Daughter, your faith has made you well. Go in peace. Be healed of your disease.

As we have worked through the early portions of Mark's Gospel, we have seen how Mark placed the short episodes with which he began his Gospel for the purpose of preparing us to see. One of those stories is the Baptism of Jesus, where Jesus, having descended into the waters of baptism (the abyss), emerged from the water. And as he did so, the heavens split open, the Spirit descended on Jesus like a dove, and the voice of God spoke: "You are my son, the one whom I love. With you, I am well pleased." We discovered that Mark placed this story at near the beginning of his Gospel to give us insight—to help us recognize what an apocalyptic moment, with the full, immediate presence of God, looks like. We then took these insights to the story of the Healing of the Paralytic, in Mark 2. And we could then see that just as the heavens split open, so did the four disciples—the four faithful followers of Christ—split open the roof of Jesus's house. And just as the Spirit descended on Jesus, so did the four men lower the paralyzed man so that he lay at the feet of Jesus.

The story of the Woman with the Hemorrhage bears similarities to these two earlier stories. There are also differences. With both the similarities and differences, Mark provides insight. The similarities bear importance: Just as the paralytic lay at the feet of Jesus, so did the woman with the hemorrhage fall at Jesus's feet. Mark is opening our eyes to another apocalyptic moment: the power of God to deliver Christ, the power by which God would raise him from the dead, was present through Christ, delivering this woman from the illness that possessed her, keeping her in exile. There is another significant apocalyptic moment that Mark has prepared us to recognize: When Jesus emerged from the waters of his baptism, the voice of God said to Jesus, "You are my son, the Beloved, with whom I am well pleased." God addresses Jesus as his son at the moment that Jesus emerges from the water. His emergence from the water prefigures his resurrection—his deliverance from death. It is worth noticing that the first time in the Bible that God addressed anyone as his son is in the fourth chapter of Exodus. The Lord spoke to Moses and said to him, "Go tell Pharaoh that Israel is *my firstborn son.*" And what did God do with his firstborn son? God delivered him from slavery and captivity in Egypt. For God to address Jesus as his son *as he emerged from the water* is for God to establish the one whom God delivers as a member of God's family.

It was in that same spirit that Jesus addressed the woman whom he had delivered from her illness. He called her daughter. He addressed her as a member of his family. This was another apocalyptic moment. The power of God was immediately present in Christ to deliver her from sickness, suffering, degradation, and exile—just as God had delivered the Israelites in the past, and just as God would deliver Christ in the future resurrection.

Thanks to Mark's genius, by the time we come to this story, we can recognize Mark's insights. The apocalyptic power of God flows from Jesus to the woman. Jesus then adopts her as a member of his family—right then and there.

Mark's ingenuity also prepares us to recognize the way in which this story *differs* from what has come before. Early in the Gospel, Jesus called four fishermen to follow him. We learned that following Christ has to do with assisting him in drawing people out of whatever abyss consumes them, placing them in the safety of the presence of God's power. In the second chapter, we saw four men implementing that calling as they brought the paralytic to Christ. Notice the way in which the story of the Woman with the Hemorrhage differs. There are no followers of Christ who are assisting him with her. They are more interested in the prestige of assisting the ruler of the synagogue. He is a man of singular importance. He's the one the disciples want to be seen with.

For all intents and purposes, the disciples leave Christ to deal with the crush of the crowd and the crushing illness of this nameless woman alone. Their lack of support, however, does not stop Jesus from offering her the most tender healing care and inclusion. Nothing will stop him from stopping for her.

As I have tried to understand the Bible over the years, I have spent time reflecting on the importance of analogy. Reading these stories involves *recognizing* what happens in these stories, *reflecting* on our own lives in light of these stories, and then finding ways to *implement* whatever insights we might gain in our own lives. Learning to see analogies involves insight into how our own circumstances are both similar and different from what we see in the stories. One of the ways I have tried to recognize and to reflect on the arts of effective analogy is through the composition of short stories. I don't mean the kind that someone like William Faulkner or Flannery O'Connor has written. I never expect to enjoy the depth of their insight, and I don't share their genius and talent. Several years ago, I did compose something to help me to see how the story of the Woman with the Hemorrhage might be reflected and perhaps even implemented in our world:

If she wanted you to stay after school, she wrote your name on the Board. And having your name written on the board meant that you were required to stay after school. Period. End of discussion.

There were twelve girls in the class. Fifth grade girls are capable of behavior that would astonish the angels. But were the truth, the whole truth, and nothing but the truth also told, it is fair to say that they are also capable of behavior that would cause the Devil to smile. This is especially true if there are eleven ten-and-a-half-year-old girls in connivance to humiliate and persecute, by whatever means they can get away with, the one unfortunate soul who became their chosen target. And this year, it was clear that it would be Maria. Why Maria?

"She flunked! Can you believe it? Ms. Creech flunked her. She's repeating Fifth Grade!" And injure Maria, they would. For what purpose? The sheer fun of cruelty.

"Not on my watch," Ms. Creech resolved within herself.

Twelve girls were in Ms. Creech's class. And she wrote eleven names on the Board. And she did so early in the day. That meant six hours of anticipation. It also meant for a much quieter day for the entire class as all were compelled to speculate as to the reason for their detainment—and also what sentence each would be under.

What happened was actually far more painful than each girl had anticipated. Perhaps to the credit of each, not one could imagine what Ms. Creech would be saying to them. Nor did they imagine with what tender kindness and mercy their teacher would speak. Ms. Creech's voice could not have been more gentle. Nor could Ms. Creech have been more direct. Everything Ms. Creech said caught them by surprise, if for no other reason than they were stunned at just how much Ms. Creech knew.

"Let me begin by telling you why Maria asked me for permission to repeat the Fifth Grade." Absolutely no one expected this for a beginning. Among other things, who could ever imagine actually asking the teacher to flunk you? It was as though Ms. Creech was reading their minds. "Notice the difference between being flunked and requesting to repeat a grade so that you can learn. As you are about to hear, Maria has taught me far more than I shall ever expect to teach her.

"You see, I prided myself on being a fine teacher—a teacher who would get the most out of her students. This of course meant that I was demanding. As you will learn, teachers should expect the best of their students, and their students will often experience this as demand.

"It is no secret that last year Maria was not a stellar student. Academically, she learned little. My frustration with Maria was endless, and I let her know in no uncertain terms. She paid little attention to my lessons—or so I fancied. Few students have been more unresponsive to my efforts at both correction and teaching than Maria. She was almost never successful at anything—preparation and homework being the most conspicuous. And if that wasn't enough, Maria was chronically tardy. And in my class, there is simply no excuse to undermine the importance of punctuality. That I demand it is for everyone's own good.

"And demand it, I did. Quietly, but with a firmness that could not be mistaken. Many a time Maria had had her name on the Board for

tardiness. Many a time we had had our quiet discussion in this very room after school. Maria had been late on a Friday. I had written her name on the Board. She had stayed after school. She had promised—promised me, mind you—that she would not be late again.

"Wouldn't you know it, on Monday morning, she was late. And not just a little late this time, but a whole two hours late.

"I exploded. Yes, I wrote her name on the Board, but not until after I had turned her ego into self-conscious mincemeat in front of my class and referred her to the office for time-out.

"At three o'clock, she came back to the room. Maria made every effort to maintain her composure. I wish I could say that I kept mine. Rage is an ugly thing. And when it's designed to humiliate another person, it is just plain evil. It is one of the moments of my life of which I am most ashamed. What more can I say? I cut her in pieces again, and I then demanded an explanation.

"Maria could keep her composure no longer. 'I'm so sorry, Ms. Creech. I told the police I couldn't be late for school. But they just wouldn't listen!'

"Maria had my attention. 'And how were you involved with the police?'

'They came to our house and arrested my mother on this morning. And after they arrested her, the police took me to the social worker, and the social worker brought me to school.'

"I was not a little incredulous. 'Why did they arrest your mother?'

'Late last night, she killed my father. Mother couldn't take it anymore. When Daddy beat her, Mother took all she could, but she couldn't take Daddy beating me. It's all so confusing, so awful. I don't know how to describe it.'

"It was then that I saw my sin. Maria's father was beating her mother, and Maria's father was beating her. And was I in tune with any of this?

"And that's not the worst of it. I had been to church the day before—the very day before. And our pastor was talking about a story of this woman in the Bible. She's bleeding inside. She's in pain. She's miserable. She's in agony. And she's silently crying out to Jesus—trying to touch him.

"Finally, one day, she touches the hem of his robe. And power flows out of Jesus into her. And the bleeding stops. And she's healed. And the pain is gone. And then the biggest miracle happens. Jesus receives her into his family. He calls her daughter. 'Daughter, your faith has made you well. Go in peace, and be healed of your disease!'

"And here's the worst part of the story. In his sermon, our pastor said, 'There is a person in your life who is bleeding inside, who is ostracized, excluded, humiliated, and in wretched misery. And that someone is crying out, perhaps silently, hoping that someone will hear and just say, "I love you; you're important to me."' The pastor said that the very day before I chewed-up Maria and spit her out."

Ms. Creech then looked at the eleven girls with understanding, sympathy, and compassion. "My abuse of her was far worse than yours. I have no moral ground from which to criticize you. I want not to do so now. But after I apologized to Maria—and apologize, I did . . ."

"Ms. Creech, tell us. Would you tell us how you apologized?"

"We don't want to be personal, Ms. Creech!"

"Thank you for asking. I first held Maria in my arms. I cried with her. I couldn't help myself. Nor should I have. It was probably the first really Christian thing I had done in my life. God knows. But *after I held her, I said, 'Maria, I am so wrong. I am totally wrong. I am so sorry. I am so very sorry. I apologize. I know you can't forgive me, . . .'*

"Maria interrupted me, looking me in the eye, and said, 'Of course I can forgive you. You're my hero. You're the reason I love coming to school! You've given me more loving attention than anyone in my life.' And she said it so quietly, without the least hint of condemnation. For Maria, there was never a question, never an internal debate about whether or not to forgive. For Maria, forgiveness was the only option.

"Do you see why? Maria knew that life—Life itself—depends on love, and love often times means forgiveness. And forgiveness is sometimes the only way to Peace. Life depends on it.

"You girls are intelligent, and I am assuming that you already understand what I mean when I say that Maria has taught me far more than I will ever teach her. I suppose that I have no business giving you my testimony, and if they fire me for it, so be it. But I resolved that day that I would be here for Maria. Not that I'd love any other child less. And not that I would not continue to challenge Maria to learn. She needs to pursue learning and truth just as much as anyone else. But I did resolve that Maria would not suffer humiliation on my watch. But then, you've already figured that out.

"Maria had the humility to know that academically, she had learned little. And because she so looked up to me, she requested the privilege of repeating my class.

"So I have called you here to ask a question: what are we going to do—together—to love Maria, to make it possible for Maria to heal and learn and grow? And what is it she's going to teach us? How are we going to learn?"

For Reflection

Where, in my life, am I reaching out trying to touch Christ? How is it that Christ is responding to me?

_____

_____

_____

Who do I know that is lost in the crush of the crowd?

_____

_____

_____

Where have I been so busy or preoccupied that I can't see others in need?

_____

_____

_____

Whom do I need to welcome into my life? With whom do I need to celebrate?

_____

_____

_____

Who needs me to stand up for them? What action am I willing to take?

_____

_____

_____

Are there relationships that I damage that I might seek healing for?

_____

_____

_____

Where do I need to offer or receive forgiveness?

_____

_____

_____

Where do I see the power of God at large in the world? What do I see the power of God doing, or accomplishing?

_____

_____

_____

Chapter 7
now you see it; now you don't

He's looking for one image that will connect or combine or
embody two points; one is a point in the concrete, and the
other is a point not visible to the naked eye, but believed
in by him firmly, just as real to him, really, as the one that
everybody sees.   —Flannery O'Connor,
                           "The Grotesque in Southern Fiction"

"Why are you talking about having no bread? Do you still
not perceive or understand? Are your hearts hardened? Do
you have eyes, and fail to see? Do you have ears, and fail
to hear? And do you not remember? When I broke the five
loaves for the five thousand, how many baskets full of broken
pieces did you collect?" They said to him, "Twelve." "And
the seven for the four thousand, how many baskets full of
broken pieces did you collect?" And they said to him, "Sev-
en." Then he said to them, "Do you not yet understand?"
                                        —Mark 8:17–21 (NRSV)

I used to have a habit that today I'm not especially proud of. If I wanted information from someone, and they didn't have that information,
I was prone to rephrase my question in an effort to manipulate, if not
coerce, information that just wasn't there. I'm sad to say that the person
I did this most to was my wife. Though I was never happy when the
information I sought was not forthcoming, in retrospect, I am sure that
I was not nearly as unhappy as was she. By the grace of God, we learn.

We recognize our mistakes, we reflect together on better ways of interacting (and treating people!), and we seek to implement improvements. The implementation process isn't perfect. Changing old patterns is like housebreaking a puppy. It takes gentle compassion and Herculean patience.

We can find ourselves in the same situation when it comes to reading stories in the Bible. It can be awfully tempting to expect a particular story to answer questions that are quite beside the point of the story. No single story contains all the answers. To overstate the situation, if you want to understand how Hamlet finds the resolve to avenge his father's death, you don't look in *Othello.* And if you want to understand the envy and duplicity of Iago, you won't find the answer in *Romeo and Juliet.* Or, if you want to know the fate of the *Starship Enterprise*, it won't help you to rent DVDs of *Star Wars*; you'll have to watch *Star Trek.* We like the idea of finding answers on demand, but the Bible doesn't work that way any more than any other piece of literature of work of art. And if my approach to a story is to demand the answer that I seek, and if the story doesn't answer *that* question, I am liable to invent answers that the story doesn't provide. I also stand to miss what the story actually tells us.

I have had occasion to study the story of the Feeding of the Five Thousand in the sixth chapter of Mark for over thirty years. This has included classes I have taught as well as classes in which I have been a student. More often than not, the question has come up, *how did Jesus do it? How did he feed the five thousand?* Speculation was then unleashed.

Was it magic? After all, Jesus had the power!

Come on, it wasn't magic. We know that miracles don't happen.

I think that Jesus motivated people to share. I think that they were hoarding their food. And once Jesus shared the five loaves and two fish, others had their consciences smitten, and they began to share as well.

I not only think you're right, I think that that's the miracle—the miracle of sharing.

But sharing isn't a real miracle. If Jesus wanted to perform a miracle, he had the power. To deny the power of miracles is just plain unfaithful!

Now, come on. If God fed five thousand people on that day because they were hungry, wouldn't God do the same thing for hungry people today? I mean, if God is merciful, and if God has the power, wouldn't it be cruel of God to allow people to starve?

So the debate has gone; so, I suspect, it will continue.

With all due respect, the reason I haven't found these debates to be fruitful is that as we defend the ideas to which we adhere with the ferocity of a mother bear protecting her cubs, we can end up pummeling each other with our positions while we level one another with accusations of mindlessness, faithlessness, ignorance, stupidity, or (horrors!) heresy. With a huff of exasperation and a sigh of superiority, we finally throw in the towel and depart for our homes, wondering why we *ever* agreed to study the Bible with *those* people, or *that* professor, in the first place when we could be doing something more productive and likely to succeed, such as finding Osama Bin Laden or getting the Palestinians and Israelis to like each other.

When studying the Bible, we find it hard to set aside our presuppositions and theories. When we do so, however, we allow the authors to show us what they saw—their unique insights. I have found this to be particularly helpful with the Feeding of the Five Thousand (in Mark 6) and its companion story, the Feeding of the Four Thousand (in Mark 8). The first of these two stories immediately follows the story of the execution and burial of John the Baptist, a story which prefigures the crucifixion and burial of Jesus. The disciples, whom Jesus has sent to teach and to cast out unclean spirits, had just returned. Jesus took them to a deserted place, where they could be alone and rest. Regrettably, this place turned out not to be as deserted as they hoped. Jesus and his disciples, finding no opportunity to rest, tried to escape by boat. This didn't work either. The crowd ran around the seashore, and when Jesus and his disciples disembarked, there they all were.

Seeing the crowd, Jesus felt compassion. He saw the chaos: they were like sheep without a shepherd. So he spent time with them and taught. As the hour grew late, Jesus's disciples suggested that he dismiss the crowd so that they could go the villages to eat. Jesus's response surprised them: "You give them something to eat." The disciples didn't have that kind of money, and even if they did, where would they find bread in such a large quantity? Jesus then asked what food they had with them. They found five loaves and two fish. Jesus directed his disciples to organize the crowd into groups. He then took the fish and the bread, lifted his eyes to heaven, blessed the bread, broke it, and gave it to his disciples to set before the people. Then follows the climax of the story: "All ate and were filled, *and they took up twelve baskets full of broken pieces and of the fish.*"

Notice Mark's focus. He didn't tell us *how* Jesus did it. His emphasis was on the baskets of broken pieces of bread. There were twelve of them. Twelve was an important number in Mark's Gospel. There were twelve disciples, just as there were twelve tribes of Israel. Twelve was the number that signaled election—the chosen people of God, those whom God called to be a light to the world. What was the significance of twelve baskets full of *broken* pieces of bread? For starters, broken bread embodied the brokenness of the body of Christ on the cross: "This is my body." When, in the story of the Feeding of the Five Thousand, Jesus took the bread, blessed and broke it, this prefigured The Supper, which embodied his arrest and crucifixion. For Mark's Gospel, broken bread symbolizes a broken body.

What, then, is Mark showing us when the disciples gathered twelve baskets of broken pieces of bread? He is showing us that if followers of Christ are to help the crowd that is in danger of drowning in hunger be fed, the followers of Christ run the risk of being broken. In other words, following Christ will not always be easy. Why? Because following Christ involves assisting him in gathering broken people and caring for their legitimate hunger and need. Early in the Gospel, Mark showed us that following Christ is like fishing; it involves assisting Christ as he casts his net into the sea and draws out those who are drowning, and helps them find their sure footing. In this story, Mark develops this idea further. Following Christ involves gathering those who are broken into the baskets of compassion, where they become a part of the community and enjoy the call and challenge of following Christ.

The story of the Feeding of the Four Thousand develops this idea further still. The stories are both similar and different. The differences are what make the stories interesting. If the stories merely duplicated each other, we would run the risk of falling asleep! In the Feeding of the Four Thousand, more emphasis is placed on Jesus's compassion and awareness of the frailty and vulnerability of the crowd: "I have compassion for the crowd, because they have been with me now for three days and have nothing to eat. If I send them away hungry to their homes, they will faint on the way—and some of them have come a great distance." Like with the first feeding story, the disciples again object to the difficulty that feeding such a crowd poses. This episode then proceeds as the first, with this difference. Here, there were *seven* loaves of bread. And at the end, they took up *seven* baskets of broken pieces.

Why the number seven? It means something different from the number twelve. Seven is the number that the Bible associates with creation. Genesis 1 contains a seven-day creation story. God executes the work of creation in six days and then rests on the seventh, the Sabbath. Seven is the number that symbolizes the creation of the whole world. As the number of universality, seven stands for *all* of creation. Mark wants us to recognize that these two stories—the Feeding of the Five Thousand with its *twelve* baskets of broken pieces, and the Feeding of the Four Thousand with its *seven*—complement each other, rendering a more complete picture, with deeper insight. The second story involves not only the elect—the chosen people of Israel, or The Twelve—but also the whole world, all people. Following Christ involves gathering both the broken of Israel and the broken of all the earth. Following Christ includes compassion both for those on the inside and for those who aren't yet on the inside.

In composing his Gospel, Mark anticipated the difficulty that we might have learning to see what he saw. Good teacher that he was, Mark didn't leave us without significant clues. Immediately following the Feeding of the Five Thousand, Jesus sent his disciples away by boat. What follows is a second story of the Calming of the Sea. This time, the disciples were alone. The wind was against them, and they were straining to make headway. Jesus then came to them, walking on the water. The disciples were terrified; they thought him to be a ghost. Jesus spoke to them gently: "Take heart, it is I; don't be afraid." Jesus then joined his disciples in the boat, and everything grew calm. Mark ends this story with an important clue that he wants us not to miss: the disciples "were utterly astounded, for they did not understand about the loaves, but their hearts were hardened" (Mark 6:51–52). Mark's insight includes a devastating indictment. To accuse the disciples of having hard hearts is to associate them with Pharaoh, king of Egypt—the one who enslaved the Hebrews and opposed Moses, as he sought to deliver the people of God from Egypt. Mark's insight is that when we refuse to recognize what it means to follow Christ in the gathering of broken pieces of bread, we run the risk of opposing Christ's involvement with the world.

Mark also knew that learning to see takes time. Although his Gospel moves more quickly than the other three Gospels, he still takes adequate time to allow us to find our focus. The second story, the Feeding of the Four Thousand, gives us a second chance. After this episode, the Pharisees asked Jesus for a sign from heaven. Their request caused Jesus to groan. Jesus and his disciples departed again by boat. Mark tells us that after they set sail, they realized that they had forgotten to bring bread. Jesus responded to their concern with a warning, "Watch out—beware of the yeast of the Pharisees and the yeast of Herod."

The disciples were confused by Jesus's response and began to wonder what on earth he was talking about. I get the impression that Jesus then began to weary of their lack of understanding: "Why are you talking about having no bread? Do you still not perceive or understand? Are your hearts hardened? Do you have eyes, and fail to see? Do you have ears, and fail to hear? And do you not remember? When I broke the five loaves for the five thousand, how many baskets full of broken pieces did you collect?"

The disciples answered, "Twelve."

Jesus continued, "And the seven for the four thousand, how many baskets full of broken pieces did you collect?"

They told him, "Seven."

Finally, Jesus asked, "Do you not yet understand?"

Over the years, I've read biblical interpreters who claim that the reason a writer such as Mark has two versions of a story is that there were two accounts of one event, probably the same event, in circulation. This line of thinking says that the author provides both accounts instead of eliminating their differences. So, for example, in the Gospel of Mark, there are two stories of the Calming of the Sea, two of the Healing of the Blind Man, two of the Feeding of the Multitude, and so on. This is not the first time in the Bible that this sort of thing happens. In the book of Genesis, there are two times when Abraham, in order to save his own skin, claims that his wife Sarah is his sister and sells her into the harem of a king. It's entirely possible that the idea that there are multiple accounts of one event is correct. There is no reason to think that one person, and one person alone, had a monopoly on events of great importance.

There is also another possibility: By giving us two accounts of similar episodes, Mark gives us the opportunity to see more—to take more in, to assimilate more insight and greater understanding. I think Mark recognized that for some of us, learning to see takes time. It's an acquired skill. For some of us, the skill comes slowly. I'm one of those. Just as I am a slow reader, I am also a slow learner. I've tried speed-reading, but when I crank-up the velocity, I don't comprehend or assimilate much. I once heard a story about a man who took a course in speed reading and then read *War and Peace* in two hours. When questioned about the novel, he said, "It's about Russia." That's about how much I'd get out of a book by Tolstoy were I to read that rapidly. When I read, I like to reflect. I like to see one part in relationship to other relevant parts of the same work, and I like to compare images and ideas between different works that address similar problems and ideas. I'm also the kind of person who learns most effectively when reviewing. I am at my best when taking a second look.

The idea of taking a second look isn't new to Mark. I know of at least one interpreter of Mark who claims that Mark got many of his ideas from Homer's *Odyssey*. Whether or not this is true, I am not qualified to say, but there are things that happen in *Odyssey* that also happen in Mark's Gospel. Two are relevant to where we are in our reflections on Mark. The first involves second looks. One of the things that make Odysseus a hero is that he learns, as a matter of practice, to take second looks. Early in the epic, Odysseus, instead of returning to an idea and reflecting on its potential results and effectiveness, would act on impulse—the moment he first had an idea. This got Odysseus into trouble and resulted in the loss of both his shipmates and his ship. Odysseus's impulsiveness also resulted in his exile and separation from home.

It was after a boatload of mistakes that practically ruined his life that Odysseus received grace: the opportunity to learn from his mistakes. One essential feature of his transformation was that Odysseus started having second thoughts. He stuck with this strategy until it became a habit. Odysseus thought up ideas with ease. When he had an idea, instead of acting on it instantly, he learned to return to the idea a second time. He pondered the potential results. He also considered at least one alternative. He considered doing *this*, and he then considered doing *that*. With both options before him, he then made his decision and acted. That's when his life started to turn around. Odysseus was headed for home.

Even so, Odysseus's homecoming wasn't immediate. The second leg of his journey home involved taking time for *reflection*. This meant that Odysseus took time for what today we would call a retreat. He went to an island that operated on a different kind of time—*kairós*. There, he revisited the significant events of his life. He told his story. He spent time in reflection. He took his past—both mistakes and failures—learned from them, and began to assimilate them into a coherent whole, which included an identity, an understanding of who he was as a human being. The combination of learning to have second thoughts and spending time in reflection set Odysseus firmly on his journey of transformation and fulfillment.

The combination of second thoughts and reflection didn't *complete* Odysseus's transformation. He still faced the difficult task of returning home and *implementing* what he had learned. But he learned—through his experience—that by returning to our experience and reflecting, we can bring sufficient order to some of the chaos that we have suffered or caused. Reflecting on and interpreting our past are essential to human transformation, growth, and excellence.

I think that Mark was fully aware of this. I also think that this is one of the reasons why he featured many of his stories in pairs. I think that Mark recognized that learning involves second looks—lots of them—and ample time for reflection. I think that Mark fully understood that some of the greatest learning involves reflection on our experience. This is what leads to the kind of insight that merits implementation.

It turns out that the center portion of Mark's Gospel (8:22—10:52) is sandwiched between two similar stories, both of which feature the healing of a blind man. Mark composed his Gospel in this way because he wanted to help us to see. Mark wanted to open our eyes to what came between the two stories of the Healing of the Blind Man. I think that Mark constructed his Gospel in this way to assist our reflections. This is what Mark wanted us to learn. This is what he wanted us to get. Mark knew this would be difficult for us. To help us understand, Mark portrayed Jesus going over the same lesson three times.

One of the things that I find fascinating about this center portion of the Gospel is how the disciples would be utterly clear about some matters while being completely clueless about others. It is as though they would get a glimpse of truths and realities that were right in front of them, and yet, at the very next moment, whatever insight they had would just slip away.

It starts off with Simon Peter. Jesus was asking what people were saying about him. He then asked The Twelve what *they* thought about him. Peter answered with resolve: "You are the Christ. You are the king of Israel!" Moreover, his answer was correct.

Now, because Peter was on the mark, I would have expected Jesus to congratulate Peter: *Wonderful! You get an A. Attaboy! I'm proud of you! You're my best disciple! Keep up the good work!* But this isn't what happens at all. Instead, Jesus teaches about the nature of his kingdom by telling The Twelve about what's going to happen to him. He says, *Look, we are going to Jerusalem, where I will be rejected, suffer, crucified, and then rise.* Mark adds that Jesus said this *plainly*—that is, openly. No parables. No cryptic or esoteric speech. Jesus's words were straightforward—as plain as plain could be.

What happens next isn't pretty. Peter begins to rebuke Jesus. Here's where it helps to remember what we have read before. Rebuking is what Jesus does to demons. When, in the first chapter, Jesus entered the synagogue, where he confronted a man possessed by an unclean spirit, Jesus *rebuked* the demon and exorcised it. By rebuking Jesus, Peter treats Jesus like a devil. Not a good idea.

The result is devastating. Jesus is not a happy camper. He turns, and eyeing all of his disciples, he rebukes Peter: "Get behind me, Satan. You are not on the side of God. You are on the side of humans!"

What's going on here? Simply put, Peter understands *that* Jesus is the Messiah (the king), but he doesn't understand *what kind of Messiah* Jesus is. Peter thinks of Jesus as a military Messiah—a mighty warrior, like King David, the greatest Messiah in the Old Testament. Like others, Peter seems to hope that Jesus will lead them in a great battle against the hated Romans, who occupy their beloved city, Jerusalem.

That isn't the kind of Messiah Jesus aspired to be. He sought to be a Messiah who confronted evil, with a goal of taking the evil out of people and out of circulation. That's why Mark features an exorcism early in his Gospel: to show us that as Messiah, Jesus comes to remove evil from us, to liberate us to do what is right.

This brings us to the all-important question, what would it mean for Christ to remove the sin and evil from us? How might we also assist Christ as he seeks to remove evil from the world in which we live? The answers to these two questions can be slippery: they involve paradox. Jesus's confrontation of his disciples' way of thinking may have seemed devastating to them. However, leaving them looking like they had barely survived a wreck was not Jesus's goal. His goal was to transform them into the full stature of their humanity by making them followers. Jesus told them that if they were serious about following him, they would have to deny themselves, take up their crosses, and follow him. The reason was equally paradoxical: those who are intent on saving their lives will lose them. Those, however, who willingly lose their lives for the sake of Christ and his gospel will find them.

What, then, would it mean to be willing to lose my life and to take up my cross? What might the contents of my reflections look like? And how might I go about implementing this vision?

I have found it to be helpful to begin by asking, what ways of thinking and living have I clung to that are unhelpful, or perhaps even destructive? What are my blind spots? What have I failed to see? What have I been up to or supported that is sinful, or perhaps even evil?

What would it mean to see? What would it mean to see things in a completely new way? What have I missed—perhaps over and over—that is right before my eyes?

What would it mean for me to live in a new way—with a new outlook, with completely new methods? What would this mean for my relationships?

What would this mean for the ways in which I conduct myself? What manners would I change? What kinds of things would I stop saying? What kinds of things would I begin to say?

What would it mean for me to become a leavening influence in the world? What would it mean for me to live with utter respect for the dignity of the person right in front of me? What would it mean for me to live for the sake of goodness and peace?

What would it mean for me to see the brokenness of others—including their pain and sorrow? What would it mean for me to embrace the brokenness of others and to stand with them? And what would it mean for me to embrace what I have shunned and avoided?

I believe that when we embrace the courage to seek answers, God opens our eyes and provides the grace. I believe that our willingness to reflect on where we have been can make an enormous difference in terms of where we go in the future. I also believe it's a journey well worth taking.

For Reflection

What stands in the way of my seeing in a completely new way? What would it mean for me to do so?

_____

_____

_____

What have I missed—perhaps over and over—that is right before my eyes?

_____

_____

_____

What would it mean for me to live in a new way—with a new outlook, with completely new methods? What would this mean for my relationships? What would this mean for the ways in which I conduct myself? What manners would I change? What kinds of things would I stop saying? What kinds of things would I begin to say?

_____

_____

_____

What would it mean for me to become a leavening influence in the world?

_____

_____

_____

What would it mean for me to live with utter respect for the dignity of the person right in front of me? What do I have to change to accomplish this? What strengths are already in place in my character and in my dealings with others?

_____

_____

_____

What would it mean for me to live for the sake of goodness and peace? What steps will I take? When will I take them? To whom will I be accountable?

_____

_____

_____

What would it mean for me to see the brokenness of others—including their pain and sorrow? What would it mean for me to embrace the brokenness of others and to stand with them? And what would it mean for me to embrace what I have shunned and avoided?

_____

_____

_____

Chapter 8
why did Jesus curse the fig tree?

He has the mistaken notion that a concern with grace is a concern with exalted human behavior, that it is a pretentious concern. It is, however, simply a concern with the human reaction to that which, instant by instant, gives life to the soul. It is a concern with a realization that breeds charity and with the charity that breeds action.

—Flannery O'Connor,
"The Catholic Novelist in the Protestant South"

If other ages felt less, they saw more, even though they saw with the blind, prophetical, unsentimental eye of acceptance, which is to say, of faith. In the absence of this faith now, we govern by tenderness. It is a tenderness which, long since cut off from the person of Christ, is wrapped in theory. When tenderness is detached from the source of tenderness, its logical outcome is terror. It ends in forced-labor camps and in the fumes of the gas chamber. —Flannery O'Connor,
"A Memoir of Mary Ann"

Truly I tell you, if you say to this mountain, "Be taken up and thrown into the sea," and if you do not doubt in your heart, but believe that what you say will come to pass, it will be done for you. —Jesus, in Mark 11:23 (NRSV)

*I*t's not the first time that we read something in Mark's Gospel that strikes us as strange. In the eighth chapter, when Jesus healed the blind man, he spit in the man's eyes. Perhaps we shouldn't be completely surprised: in the seventh chapter, when Jesus healed the man who suffered from deafness and an impediment in speech, Jesus placed his fingers in the man's ears and then spat on the man's tongue. These methods, to be blunt, are rather bizarre. They certainly don't fall into the category of what we would expect.

In the same spirit, I confess that I find Jesus's cursing of the fig tree to be a bit odd. Why would Mark include such a story? What was he trying to show us?

The eleventh chapter of Mark, where this episode appears, marks a significant turning point in the Gospel—the final phase in Jesus's ministry, the place where Jesus *implements* his vision of the kingdom of God. This final phase of the Gospel contains significant teaching. Jesus wasn't at a loss for words. He had plenty to say. But the implementation of his vision also involved lots of action. The kingdom of God does not consist of mere words. Mark portrayed Jesus teaching with authority, but he didn't portray Jesus as mere teacher. He presented Jesus exercising power. It was a certain *kind* of power. It wasn't the violent force of a warrior king charging into battle. But neither was it weak and ineffectual. It was a power remarkable for its strength, but its remarkability lay in its capacity to effect goodness and peace. Strangely, this vision of the power of God included cursing the fig tree.

The implementation of Jesus's vision of God's kingdom began with his entry into Jerusalem. The significance of this event lay in the *manner* by which Jesus made his entrance. From Bethphage, to the east of Jerusalem, Jesus directed his disciples to enter the city, where they would find a young donkey that had never been ridden. They were to untie the colt and bring it to Jesus. On this animal, Jesus rode into Jerusalem. As he made his way, a large crowd welcomed him, honoring him with leafy branches as they shouted, "Hosanna! Blessed is he who comes in the name of the Lord! Blessed is the coming kingdom of our ancestor David! Hosanna in the highest heaven!" The exclamation of Hosanna means, *Lord save us, we pray!* It is worth noting that the way in which they cheered for Jesus spoke volumes of their hopes and expectations. Their ancestor, King David, was the greatest warrior king of Israel's history, and many of the people wanted Jesus to lead a battle that would deliver Jerusalem from Roman control. They envisioned his doing so the conventional way—with violence. This expectation is reflected in their prayer.

This expectation completely missed the significance of what Jesus sought to implement. In the ninth chapter of Zechariah, the prophet wrote that when God's Messiah returned to Jerusalem, the people would recognize his intentions by observing the manner of his entry into the city. If he rode on a war horse, we would know that he had come to fight. But if he rode on a donkey, we would know that he had come to make peace.

It isn't difficult to imagine what Zechariah meant by this. The idea of a warrior's riding into battle on a donkey is laughable. We have only to imagine something like knights in shining armor facing off and charging each other on donkeys to get a glimpse of the insight that Zechariah conveyed. For Jesus to ride into the city on a donkey was for him to embody the actions of a peacemaker.

Every one of Jesus's actions bore significance. When Jesus made his entrance into Jerusalem, he went straight to the Temple where he took a look, but he wasn't yet ready to act. On this first day, Jesus was gathering intelligence, sizing-up the situation. When he finally acted, he wanted to act decisively, with results clearly in mind. Jesus's actions would be completely premeditated. The hour was also late, so Jesus left the Temple for Bethany, which is a couple of miles to the east of Jerusalem.

On the following day, Jesus took action. From Bethany, he headed straight for the Temple in Jerusalem. In the distance, Jesus saw a fig tree. When he approached it, he found nothing on the tree but leaves. There was no fruit because it was out of season. In response to this situation, Jesus cursed the fig tree: "May no one ever eat fruit from you again."

Following the cursing of the fig tree, Jesus again entered the Temple to take decisive action. There, he confronted those whom he had apparently seen on the previous day—people who were using the Temple to turn a profit. Jesus's action was anything but weak and indecisive. He drove out everyone who exploited the Temple for personal gain: "Is it not written, 'My house shall be called a house of prayer for all the nations'? But you have made it a den of robbers."

The crowd in the Temple was spellbound by Jesus's words and actions. But some of those present—the chief priests and the scribes—took offense at what Jesus both did and said. They wanted to find a way to get rid of Jesus once and for all. However, given his effect on the people, they were afraid of him.

The next morning, Jesus and his disciples passed the tree that Jesus had cursed. The disciples were astonished to find it completely withered. Jesus's response to them was almost cryptic. Almost, but not quite: "Have faith in God. Truly I tell you, if you say to this mountain, 'Be taken up and thrown into the sea,' and if you do not doubt in your heart, but believe that what you say will come to pass, it will be done for you."

What did Jesus mean by this? And what did this strange claim have to do with cursing the fig tree? They were, in fact, related. The mountain to which Jesus referred, which would be taken up and thrown into the sea (that is, the abyss), was the Temple mount. Jesus was making a prophetic statement about the destruction of the Temple in Jerusalem. Its being destroyed would be the result of the judgment of God. This was also the meaning of the cursing of the fig tree: it was a metaphor for the cursing of the Temple.

The images of the cursing of the fig tree and the Temple mount being thrown into the sea capture our attention. They are both strange, and their strangeness makes them intriguing. That Mark's images strike us as outlandish or odd causes us to pause. At least, this causes me to pause! It raises an important question, why does Mark write this way? What does he want us to see?

Mark used a particular literary method. Fortunately, Mark's method of writing isn't difficult to grasp. More fortunate still, the payoff for taking some time to understand his method is rich. Mark's literary technique goes by the fancy name of *chiasmus*. It's a simple concept; it isn't something we need to feel intimidated by. I tell my students, "If you want to know what a chiasmus is, think Oreo Cookie." An Oreo Cookie is a kind of hybrid: it's a cross between a cookie (what in England is called a biscuit) and a sandwich. A sandwich consists of two slices of bread, between which are placed the goodies—the meat, lettuce, tomato, mayonnaise, and the like. An Oreo Cookie is a kind of sandwich. Between two slices of cake is the cream filling—the part that makes the Oreo Cookie tasty. Watch a child eat an Oreo

Cookie. She will take the cookie apart and eat the cream filling first. Why? Because the cream filling is the best part. If you don't believe me, just ask the child! Afterward, she may or may not eat the cake. For children, what's in the middle is what the cookie is all about. That's what the child most enjoys. The cream filling is the sweetest.

A chiasmus is like an Oreo Cookie. It is a literary form, *A-B-A*. The story will open with an *A*-section, move to the *B*-section, and then return to the *A*-section, with which the story concludes. Earlier, for example, we looked at the story of the Woman with the Hemorrhage (in Mark 5). This was the story of the woman who had been hemorrhaging for twelve years, and as a consequence of her condition, she was regarded as ceremonially unclean. Uncleanness resulted in ostracism from the family of God. The person who was chronically unclean lived essentially in exile. The woman had also heard about Jesus and his healing. From the within the crowd that surrounded Jesus, she reached out and touched the hem of his garment. Power flowed from Jesus to the woman and delivered her from her bleeding. Finally, Jesus addressed her as a member of his family, welcoming her into the kingdom of God.

As the *B*-section of a chiasmus, the story of the Woman with the Hemorrhage is the cream filling of the story that surrounds it: the Healing of the Daughter of the Ruler of the Synagogue. The *A*-section began when Jairus, the ruler, approaches Jesus. Jairus's twelve-year-old daughter was sick to the point of death. Jairus begged Jesus so come and to lay hands on his daughter. It was as Jesus was on his way to heal Jairus's daughter that Jesus healed the woman of her twelve-year-old hemorrhage. This was the *B*-section of the story. The *A*-section resumes as Jesus continued to Jairus's home where he encountered the girl whom he proclaimed not to be dead, but sick. Jesus then took her by the hand and said, *Talitha Cum*, which means, *little girl, arise!* The girl did as Jesus commanded. She was healed of her disease.

The parts of the chiasmus work together. The heart of the chiasmus—its guts, so to speak—is the *B*-section. This is the cream filling that provides the meaning of the entire story. To put it another way, the *B*-section opens our eyes to the meaning and significance of the *A*-section. The *A*-section, for example, raises the question: "What will it take for the children of the synagogue (the chosen people of God, signified by the number twelve) to be transformed and raised to new life?" The answer is found in the *B*-section, where the woman is healed of her twelve year bleeding, from which she is delivered and finally restored as a member of the family of God. Mark wants us to see that the family of God comes to greater fulfillment as the sick and the outcasts are delivered and returned from exile—just as the Israelites were delivered from slavery and brought to the Promised Land. Mark helps us to see this by using the literary form of the chiasmus, something he does several times throughout his Gospel.

The largest chiasmus in the Gospel is the middle section (8:22—10:52). The two stories of the Healing of the Blind Man form the *A*-sections. In the *B*-section, we find the heart of what Mark wants us to see. This is the place where Jesus teaches his disciples about his rejection, suffering, death, and resurrection. The disciples have such great difficulty with what Jesus is trying to teach them that he must go over the lesson three times. One of the things I find fascinating about Mark's writing is that Jesus's first lesson about his death and resurrection is followed by the story of his Transfiguration— the second major apocalyptic story in his Gospel (the first is Jesus's baptism; the third I will address below). In this story, which is in the ninth chapter of Mark, Jesus takes Peter, James, and John to the top of a mountain, where Jesus is transformed. His clothing becomes dazzling white, and the prophets Moses and Elijah appear with Jesus in conversation. Mark doesn't tell us the contents of the conversation. He does, on the other hand, tell us that Peter suggested that they make three booths for the three prophets (like Moses and Elijah, Jesus was a prophet). Mark also tells us that the reason Peter makes this suggestion is that he doesn't know what to say. In other words, Peter just plain doesn't understand.

Why doesn't Mark tell us what Jesus and the other two prophets are talking *about*? And what is it that Peter has such difficulty understanding? Like everything else in Mark's extraordinary Gospel, the answer is right before our eyes. We can see it in the way Mark composes his Gospel: The transfiguration of Jesus immediately follows Jesus's teaching about the necessity and importance of his rejection, suffering, and death. The placement of the Transfiguration story, along with the presence of the great prophets Moses and Elijah, are no accident. The Transfiguration ratifies Jesus's teaching: it opens our eyes to the authenticity of what Jesus is teaching by allowing us to see that Jesus's teaching fits the heart of an apocalyptic world. The fact that there is no meaningful dialogue between Jesus, Moses, and Elijah serves as a foil to the dialogue that had just taken place between Jesus and his disciples. To put it another way, the lack of dialogue between Jesus and the two prophets reflects our attention back to the dialogue between Jesus and his disciples. The meaning that merits our reflection is embodied in Jesus's teaching about his cross and resurrection, including the challenging paradox of taking up our crosses and following him.

There's more: Just as the story of the Transfiguration ratifies and supports all that Jesus has just taught, so will the resurrection of Jesus from the dead ratify Jesus's willingness to risk rejection and suffering. Jesus's crucifixion embodies the transformative power of God. Where Jesus willingly withheld violence, God's power was fully present. To put it another way, Jesus's willingness to withhold violence bore the capacity to hold God's power.

Remarkably, it was necessary for Jesus to embrace this truth as an act of faith. Doing so—especially through his suffering—involved the greatest of risk. Risk means that there are no guarantees. This was why Jesus, as he hung in agony on the cross, pled with God: "Why have you forsaken me?" The choice to suffer was entirely Jesus's own. This was not something that God could have coerced from him: any hint of coercion would have completely undermined the capacity for the cross to bear the transformative power of God. To add to the risk, the reality of the presence of the power of God in and through our greatest vulnerability is not something that can be entirely explained. It must be embodied and lived to be known: *If any would be my disciples, let them deny themselves, take up their cross, and follow me. For those who would save their lives will lose them. But those who lose their lives for my sake will find them.*

Ambiguity is a necessary consequence of paradox. This means that there is ample room for human reflection and choice. God does not determine everything ahead of time. We are free to respond both to our circumstances and to God's presence in them. We are free either to see or to close our eyes. We are at liberty either to understand or to remain in the abyss of our illusions. We have choice aplenty—the capacity for recognition, reflection, and choice. The fact that there is risk—the fact that there are no guarantees—affords us both the privilege and responsibility to rise to the full stature of human dignity. Our lives on earth have limits, but within those limits, we enjoy enormous freedom to live, move, and act as full, authentic members of the family of God.

This brings us back to the puzzle with which we started: Why did Jesus curse the fig tree? Mark pointed out that it wasn't the season for figs. For Jesus to curse the fig tree when it was out of season would at first seem less than reasonable. But since the fig tree stands as a metaphor for the Temple, which is what Jesus was really, finally, and ultimately cursing, Mark is finally claiming that the Temple itself was out of season, out of date. The Temple had ceased to bear fruit—like the fig tree.

Though not bearing fruit, this fig tree still had its leaves. And the fact that it is a fig tree reminds us of the story of Adam and Eve: when they had taken the one *and only* fruit that God had not offered them, they used fig leaves to conceal their nakedness. With an allusion to Eden, is Mark suggesting that the Temple, like the fig tree in the Garden of Eden, was functioning as an institution of concealment instead of effecting forgiveness and healing? In other words, had not the temple ceased to restore and to incorporate people into the family of God?

Notice what happens when we observe that the Cleansing of the Temple is the *B*-section of a chiasmus (like the story of the Woman with the Hemorrhage). Is Mark not suggesting that just as the woman was hemorrhaging—and had been in this condition for years—so is the Temple, owing to its ineffectiveness, its being completely out of season, hemorrhaging as well? And when Jesus then suggests a faith that will move a mountain—the mountain on which the Temple is built—and cast it into the sea, is he not also suggesting that because the Temple has ceased effecting forgiveness, restoration, and incorporation into the family of God, it will be thrown into the abyss?

What clues does Mark give for us to answer this question? The third, final, and largest apocalyptic story in the Gospel is found in the thirteenth chapter of Mark. This is the place where Jesus speaks about the destruction of the Temple in Jerusalem by Roman armies, which took place in the year 70. In Mark's Gospel, Jesus speaks about this event apocalyptically. It's worth remembering from the first two apocalyptic stories that Mark includes them because he wants us to learn how to see the apocalyptic nature of the most significant events of history.

In speaking about the destruction of the Temple, Jesus characterizes it as *desolating sacrilege.* It's another of those claims that Mark wants to make sure that we thoroughly (or at least, sufficiently!) understand. Jesus's statement alludes to the book of Daniel, and it goes like this: "But when you see the desolating sacrilege set up where it ought not to be (let the reader understand), then those in Judea must flee to the mountains; the one on the house-top must not go down or enter the house to take anything away; the one in the field must not turn back to get a coat. Woe to those who are pregnant and to those who are nursing infants in those days! Pray that it may not be in winter." One of the many things about this statement that are interesting is Mark's parenthetical admonishment, *let the reader understand.* I don't think that Mark would have exhorted us this way had he not anticipated the difficulty we would have understanding what Jesus was saying here. Now, in its original context in Daniel, the *desolating sacrilege* refers to the setting up of a pagan idol on the Temple, which the book of Daniel talks about at length.

The desolating sacrilege of which Mark's Gospel speaks is clearly pagan in origin. It specifically refers to the destruction of the Temple by pagan Romans in the year 70. We have Luke to thank for our ability to understand what Mark wanted us to see. Perhaps Luke was less confident than Mark that his readers would get the point. In the twenty-first chapter of his Gospel, Luke translates Mark's meaning. The result is the elimination of any ambiguity that might be the cause of our misunderstanding. Luke's Jesus puts it this way: "When you see Jerusalem surrounded by armies, then know that its desolation has come near." Luke is prosaic and blunt, and I for one am grateful. The desolating sacrilege is the destruction of the Temple. That is the moment of the liberation of the people of God. That was when the followers of Jesus were to run for their lives.

Mark has brought us right into the mystery of what it means to live in the kingdom of God—as a member of God's family. In involves recognition—a life spent learning to see. It involves taking time to reflect on our own capacities to act and to bear the power of God that is given to us. It involves coming to terms with the risks that are a part of our most authentic humanity. It involves embracing the ambiguity and paradox that lie at the heart of human freedom. And it involves taking responsibility and making choices—acting on the grace given to us to see, the fruits of our reflection to live and move, and the capacity we have to bear God's power. To state it a bit more simply, it involves the freedom to implement the fruits of our thoughtful reflection.

In the kingdom of God, the power that raised Christ from the dead is the same power that delivered and restored the woman with the hemorrhage, withered the accursed fig tree, and delivered the followers of Christ from a Temple that had ceased to incorporate people into God's family. This is the same power that Christ calls us to risk embracing and implementing in our own lives. With both risk and implementation, we rise to the full stature of our humanity.

For Reflection

Jesus's actions towards the Temple were decisive. At the same time, he didn't act with haste, but deliberation. How am I when it comes to implementation? Do I take sufficient time for reflection? Do I take the right amount of time to prepare? And when it comes to acting, do I rush? Do I procrastinate?

_____

_____

_____

How am I when it comes to decisiveness? Do I get stuck? Do I measure my actions appropriately, with an eye towards the best results?

_____

_____

_____

When it comes to moving mountains, what kind of mountains have I faced in the past? What was my attitude? How did I act? What were the results?

_____

_____

_____

What kind of mountain do I face now? What needs to move? What might I do to collaborate with Christ to move that mountain? When will I act?

_____

_____

_____

Where is Christ calling on me to act as peacemaker? In order to assist him in making peace, how will I act? Will I act decisively? How will I combine decisiveness with self-restraint? What will that look like?

_____

_____

_____

Some of those who encountered Christ took offense. Do I take offense? Am I a person easily offended? If so, why? What kind of person is Christ calling and challenging me to be? How will I respond?

_____

_____

_____

Where do I try to save my life? What would it mean for me to lose (some of) my life for the sake of Christ and his gospel?

_____

_____

_____

What kinds of risks might Christ call on me to take as I seek to interact with others in the interest of peace? What would it mean for me to deny myself, take up my cross, and follow Christ?

_____

_____

_____

What am I willing to do to live as a member of Christ's family?

_____

_____

_____

Chapter 9 ∽
the great transformation

The Southern writer is forced from all sides to make his gaze extend beyond the surface, beyond mere problems, until it touches that realm which is the concern of prophets and poets. —Flannery O'Connor,
"The Grotesque in Southern Fiction"

Most of us have learned to be dispassionate about evil, to look it in the face and find, as often as not, our own grinning reflections with which we do not argue, but good is another matter. Few have stared at that long enough to accept the fact that its face too is grotesque, that in us the good is something under construction.

—Flannery O'Connor, "A Memoir of Mary Ann"

If the writer believes that our life is and will remain essentially mysterious, if he looks upon us as beings existing in a created order to whose laws we freely respond, then what he sees on the surface will be of interest to him only as he can go through it into an experience of mystery itself. His kind of fiction will always be pushing its own limits outward toward the limits of mystery, because for this kind of writer, the meaning of a story does not begin except at a depth where adequate motivation and adequate psychology and the various determinations have been exhausted. Such a writer will be interested in what we don't understand rather than in what we do. —Flannery O'Connor,
"The Grotesque in Southern Fiction"

While he was at Bethany in the house of Simon the leper, as he sat at the table, a woman came with an alabaster jar of very costly ointment of nard, and she broke open the jar and poured the ointment on his head. —Mark 14:3 (NRSV)

It was over twenty-five years ago that I began trying to understand Mark's Gospel. The final three chapters (14–16) are known as The Passion. There was no passage in the Bible that haunted me more. It was one of those stories that seemed to contain great mystery. Moreover, it seemed to be a mystery that merited study and reflection.

Years later, I would finally understand that although there is much in Mark's Gospel that we could understand rationally, there is still much—perhaps more—mystery that I would have to live and experience. I will never understand all of Mark's mystery exhaustively, any more than I will finally and *completely* understand my wife Nancy, or our children Jaime and David. Do I feel like I know them? Yes. Am I justified in that feeling? I think so, and I think they would agree. But knowing them well, even knowing them better than most people will ever know them, does not mean knowing everything about them. In the same spirit, I can know much about Mark's Passion, but this does not mean that I know all that there is to know, or that I ever will.

One of the characteristics of a *great* work of literature is that we keep coming back to it. There is so much in there that every time we return to it, it yields more. We see more, we understand more, we take in more. We might even say that our earlier efforts to understand a work enlarge our capacities for understanding, rendering the return readings all the more rewarding.

I hope I am justified in saying that Mark's Passion was the single story that began to teach me to learn to see. I intend this as an important claim, but a modest one nevertheless. I am under no illusion that I see it all, that I know it all, or that I ever will. And I'm not one of those tiresome teachers who believe that the only way anyone will ever come to full, legitimate insight into Mark's Gospel is to read my books or to listen to me lecture. I do, however, find Mark's insights to be utterly fascinating and important. For me, they are compelling because they ring true. Ultimately, however, no one should have to take my word for it—or anyone else's, for that matter. The proof of the pudding is in the eating, and here, the word *proof* means *test*.

One of those insights came from the opening episode, the story of the Anointing of Jesus, in the fourteenth chapter. In this story, many puzzle-pieces come together. The story is framed by the plot of the chief priests and the scribes: they want Jesus to be killed, but they want to conceal their actions, keeping their role in the plot a secret. To say that their plot frames the Anointing is to recognize that their plotting to kill Jesus, along with the story of Jesus's anointing, form a chiasmus. The plot to kill Jesus is the *A*-section, and the anointing is the *B*-section. One of Mark's insights is that a large part of their motive for wanting to eliminate Jesus can be found in the *B*-section.

The story is straightforward. Jesus was not in Jerusalem, but in Bethany. And he was at the home not of Simon Peter, but Simon the Leper. This in itself was remarkable. He wasn't with one of his chief disciples; he was with a leper. Moreover, he was at table in the leper's home, enjoying his hospitality. Lepers, of course, were unclean. Like the woman with the hemorrhage, lepers were kept in exile. Anyone or anything that a leper touched became unclean. This is not the first time that Jesus has had contact with a leper. At the end of the first chapter of Mark, a leper approached Jesus and said, "I know that you *can* make me clean. Are you willing?" Jesus was willing. He also reached out and *touched* the leper.

The story of the Anointing carries Jesus's involvement with the leper a step further: here, Jesus became the guest in a leper's home, placing himself in the leper's care. By doing this, Jesus became the guest of an outcast—or in biblical terms, the guest of an exile.

As Jesus and Simon the leper enjoyed the relationship between guest and host, a woman entered Simon's house, carrying a jar of expensive oil. The oil was worth three hundred *denarii*, which means three hundred day's wages. The woman took the jar, broke it open, and poured the oil over Jesus's head.

For reasons that Mark doesn't tell us, there were others present who witnessed the woman's anointing of Jesus. These others raised objections: they claimed that the extravagant use of such costly oil was a reckless waste. The oil (went their reasoning) should have been sold and the proceeds given to the poor. Jesus, however, knew their concern for the poor to be a smoke-screen: They wanted Jesus out of the picture, but they didn't want to take (public) responsibility for their motives or their actions. Jesus confronted their duplicity: You will always have the poor with you, and you can help them *whenever you are willing*. If they were willing, they would do so. The proof was in the implementation.

Jesus then made a claim that was as extraordinary as the woman's actions. He characterized what the woman had done as beautiful: *she has anointed his body beforehand for burial*. What did Jesus mean by this? And why is it significant? On the surface, this is the one and only time in the entire Gospel that Jesus was anointed. After his crucifixion, there was no time to prepare his body for burial: it was the Sabbath, and no work was allowed. There is, however, deeper significance to this anointing. The word *Messiah* means *anointed one*, as does the word *Christ*. *Messiah* is from the Hebrew language, and *Christ* is from the Greek. Both mean the same thing. In Israel, the Messiah was the *anointed king*. David, for example, formally became *king of Israel* when the prophet Samuel *poured oil over his head*.

In what sense, though, has the woman anointed Jesus *for burial*? It pays to remember that in the time of Jesus, a woman had no social standing. A woman was not allowed to bear witness. Women were decidedly subordinate. The culture was patriarchal. It was run by the men. Notice, however, what this woman has done. In the first place, she has acted as a fully legitimate member of the royal family of God. She has even acted as a prophet (like the prophet Samuel). This woman has taken full responsibility for anointing Jesus as Messiah, king of Israel. Notice *the place* where she has anointed Jesus—not in Jerusalem, where we would expect the Messiah to be anointed, but in Bethany, of all places! And if that weren't a sufficient affront, she has anointed Jesus while he is a guest in the home of a leper—an exile, one who is an outcast from the conventional people of God.

As we begin to grasp what the woman accomplished by anointing Jesus Messiah, we would do well to observe what an anthropologist would call *the obvious aspects of anointing*: Oil is a lubricant. A lubricant facilitates contact between two bodies with less friction. By anointing Jesus, while he was the guest in the home of Simon the leper in Bethany, this woman was bearing witness that *as Messiah, Jesus reduces the friction with which women, lepers, and other social outcasts had been kept in exile from the kingdom of God.*

This woman was also taking responsibility for transforming and redefining the *nature* of the kingdom of God. In the kingdom which Jesus implements, and for which he stands, not only are women and lepers included, but they are instrumental in its design. By the decision of this woman, the family of God is no longer centered in Jerusalem. It is now centered in Bethany, in the home of a leper (or, if it is not centered in Bethany, the leper's home in Bethany is at least *one* of its centers). Moreover, the leper is no longer a nameless outcast; his name is Simon, and Simon is also the name of one of Jesus's chief disciples, Simon Peter. Jesus is guest in this Simon's home, and it is *there* that he formally becomes Messiah.

As far as *this* Messiah was concerned, for a woman to assume responsibility for both anointing him and at the same time transforming the constitution of God's kingdom was beautiful. Jesus says so, and he says so without ambiguity. This time, when Jesus speaks, there is no paradox. The meaning is right there for all to see. For Jesus, however, to characterize his anointing as "beautiful" is for him to accept the death that he will most surely die. By accepting *this* anointing, Jesus was confronting and offending everything for which conventional authorities stood.

Those who took offense at what Jesus, the woman, and Simon accomplished together would see to it that Jesus got what he had coming. Their *way* of seeing to it was the consequence of their *unwillingness to see* and to embrace the kingdom for which Jesus stood, a kingdom that to a large degree was being defined by those who had been its outcasts. As the Passion continued, Mark would not only help us to recognize actions which Jesus's enemies would subsequently conceal, but he would do so in a way that would urge *us* to ponder *our* possible opposition to the kingdom that this woman was in part redesigning.

When we looked at the story of Jesus's transfiguration, we noticed that in the Gospel of Mark, what *isn't* said is sometimes as significant at what *is* said. Perhaps more than any other story, Mark's passion opens our eyes to what isn't said. The episode is the Preparation for the Celebration of the Passover (in Mark 14). The instructions that Jesus gave his disciples bear some similarity to the instructions Jesus gave his disciples to fetch the donkey that he would ride into Jerusalem (Mark 11). What is striking about the instructions Jesus gave for the preparation of the meal is that they tell us so little (or withhold so much). Jesus told his disciples to go into the city. Which city? We assume that he meant Jerusalem. I'm not sure that they would have considered Bethany large enough to be a full-blown city, but *we can't be entirely sure*. Jesus then said that they would find a man carrying a jar of water. This may have been unusual in that carrying water was probably women's work. This would mean that the disciples would have no difficulty spotting him. What is also interesting is that Mark didn't specify the man's identity. Instead, Jesus directed the disciples simply to follow the man, who would lead them to a house. They were to enter the house, where they would meet the owner. Jesus didn't specify his name either. The disciples were to say to the owner, "The Teacher asks, Where is my guest room where I may eat the Passover with my disciples?" The owner would then show them a large room that was furnished and ready. Everything would be in order.

What is so intriguing, if not odd, about this story? There is so much secrecy involved: Jesus doesn't specify the name of the city, the contact, the location of the house, or the name of the owner. He doesn't even tell us—for sure—if the upper room, which they will find furnished and ready, is located in that particular house. Why does Mark withhold so much information? I would like to suggest that he is looking for a certain effect. The air of secrecy creates an atmosphere of conspiracy. It includes unnamed contacts in undisclosed locations. That is where the disciples will make their preparations.

It is during this meal that Mark prepares us to recognize the transformation that lies at the heart of the kingdom that Jesus implements. During the meal, Jesus took bread, blessed it, broke it, gave it to his disciples and said, "Take, this is my body." Jesus then took the cup, gave thanks, gave it to them and said, "This is my blood of the covenant, which is poured out for many. Truly I tell you, I will never again drink of the fruit of the vine until that day when I drink it new in the kingdom of God" (Mark 14:24–25).

At the beginning of this essay, I acknowledged that there is much about The Passion that we can understand, but there is also much that we will never fully understand in this life. Jesus's taking bread, breaking it, and saying, "Take, this is my body," is one such passage. In sharing what I believe to be one of Mark's stunning insights into the nature of the kingdom of God,

I do not mean to claim that there are not also other insights of import with reference to the Lord's Supper.

To open our eyes to the obvious aspects of the story, we can't help but notice two things. The first is that Jesus calls the bread *his body*. The second is that what Jesus does with the bread bears similarity to Jesus's conduct when they arrest him in the Garden of Gethsemane. To put it another way, there is an analogy between what Jesus does with the bread in the supper and the way he responds to those who take him. To recognize an analogy between the two situations and actions is to observe that they are both similar and different. They are not identical actions in identical circumstances, but their similarities are strikingly acute and of incalculable import.

At the moment when they come for Jesus, his conduct is remarkable not only for what it accomplishes, but also for what it avoids—for what Jesus *doesn't* do. Jesus neither retaliates nor flees. Jesus doesn't *fight for his life*, nor does he *run and hide*. Given the location of the Garden of Gethsemane, *flight* would have been just as much an option as *fight*. Jesus could have escaped up the Mount of Olives towards Bethany to the east. From there, he could easily have made his way to the hills of Judea. Flight may not have been an attractive option, but it was a realistic option. More heroic (at least conventionally speaking) would have been for Jesus to *stand up and fight like a man!* These were the options that Jesus rejected.

What Jesus *did* was almost more than we can take in and comprehend: Jesus presented himself to his captors. *Jesus transformed his own being taken into a gift.* He transformed their act of taking into an act of receiving. Moreover, Mark also helps us to see that similarity between transforming his own being taken into a gift on the one hand and what Jesus does with the bread in The Supper on the other: with the bread, which Jesus himself breaks, Jesus says, *Take, this is my body.*

What is the connection between these two crucial events? What is the *transformation* that Jesus is *implementing*? What is the transformation that Mark wants *us* to recognize, to ponder, and to implement in our lives? Mark wants us to see that Jesus's Passion contains yet another transformation that lay at the heart of the kingdom of God. *This* transformation addresses the ways in which we resolve conflict. It recognizes a human tendency to see two potential solutions when faced with serious conflict—fight or flight. When trouble brews, our impulse is either to retaliate or to run.

The kingdom that Jesus the Messiah implemented recognized that our *impulse* does not always embody the full dignity of our humanity. Impulse comes quickly and involuntarily, without reflection or forethought. The problem is that the consequences of impulses hastily acted on are not always good, constructive, or desirable. When Jesus takes bread, blesses it, breaks it, and gives it to us, saying, *This is my body*, he is compelling us, as members of his family in God's kingdom, to reflect mindfully on the question, *given our circumstances, what would it mean to transform our own being taken into a gracious gift? What might such action look like? What might result? What are the probable outcomes? What are the possible outcomes? What are potential consequences? What can we know about the risks? What is the cost of transformation? What is the cost of running away? What is the cost of retaliation?*

For Jesus, implementing this transformation cost him dearly. Jesus also recognized that retaliating with haste has a cost. So does abandonment. Jesus knew that although conventional wisdom says that flight is cowardly, and fight takes courage, transforming our being taken into a gracious presence takes more courage still. For Jesus to implement such a vision was almost unbearable. For his disciples, it was more than they were willing to bear. It wasn't something they even wished to entertain as a possibility. We see this in the episodes that surround Jesus's arrest with the great transformation in the Garden. Jesus found the mere idea of going through with his vision—taking it all the way to the cross—to be overwhelming. I find the prayer that Jesus prays in the Garden to be heartbreaking: "Abba, Father, for you all things are possible; remove this cup from me; yet, not what I want, but what you want." This is not the prayer of a man who looks forward to the torture that he will suffer.

All that Jesus had requested of Peter, James, and John was that they watch—keep awake—as Jesus prayed. For whatever reason, even that was more than they were willing to do. Three times, Jesus found them sleeping. *Could you not keep awake for even an hour?* And when Jesus was on trial in the Temple, before the High Priest, Simon Peter was in the courtyard of the Temple. Three times, one of the servant-girls of the high priest accused Peter of association with Jesus. Peter vehemently denied any link to Jesus. On his third denial, Peter effectually said, *A curse be on me if Jesus and I have ever had anything to do with each other.*

We have already seen something of the significance of the number *three* in Mark's Gospel. Between the two stories of the Healing of the Blind Man, Jesus found it necessary to go over the importance of his suffering, death, and resurrection *three times.* Similarly, the disciples sleep through Jesus's prayer *three times.* Finally, Peter denies Jesus *three times* as well. I think that Mark wanted us to see the connection between these threes and the final three hours of Jesus's death on the cross. After Jesus's two trials—one before the high priest, the other before Pilate—they crowned Jesus with thorns, placed a purple (royal) robe on him, saluted him as *King of the Jews*, mocked him, spat on him, stripped him, put his own clothing back on him, and crucified him. When they did so, they posted the charge, *King of the Jews.* Mark's insight, in other words, was that they crucified him *because* he was the Messiah. He was a Messiah who welcomed the woman as a designer of his kingdom. He was a Messiah who accepted the hospitality of a leper. He was a Messiah who dared transform his own being taken into a gracious gift, with the audacious call to take up our cross and to follow him. This was what Jesus implemented willingly. This is what most of his own disciples wanted nothing to do with: *They all forsook him and fled.* This is the kingdom for which he gave his life.

On the occasion of the crucifixion, Mark specifies the final set of threes. They are cosmic in nature. They involve a reference to time: Jesus's crucifixion spanned the third hour, the sixth hour, and the ninth hour—nine o'clock in the morning, high noon, and three o'clock in the afternoon. Mark recognized that the kingdom Jesus dared to implement touched the entire cosmos. Its effect was apocalyptic. It was an action that reverberated throughout the entire universe for all time. It left nothing untouched, nothing unaffected.

It was a real death—a real crucifixion in time and place. Jesus's crucifixion was the ultimate transformation. That is because of the presence of the power by which God then raised Jesus from the dead. The resurrection ratified the crucifixion, completing it as the ultimate transformation of all life for all time. Taken together, the cross and resurrection of Jesus from the dead constitute the transformative event in time and space that permeates and addresses all circumstances in all places at all times. They leave no situation unaddressed; nothing untouched. The possibility for peace and wholeness are more clear and more present in the cross and resurrection than anything of which the human heart can conceive or the human mind imagine. This event is the criterion, the standard, and the means of transformation and of life. This is the ultimate apocalyptic event. This kingdom, which the woman helped design and which Jesus transformed, embodies the fullness of human dignity and the power of God.

At the heart of the mystery of Christ's transformation is his resurrection from the dead. Here, the power of God fulfills, ratifies, and brings to completion everything Jesus taught, stood for, and dared to implement. Mark recognized that even the promise of resurrection and the presence of the power of God do not completely eliminate the risks and dissolve the fear. The Passion begins with a woman's taking responsibility for determining some of the shape that the kingdom of God will take. At the end of the story, the three women flee the tomb in terror. They went to the tomb expecting to embalm Jesus's corpse. Instead, they found a young man dressed in white, who told them that Jesus had been raised from the dead. The young man directed the women to tell Jesus's disciples—including Peter, who denied Jesus—that Jesus was going before them to Galilee. He would meet them there.

What is Mark showing us? The implementation of the kingdom of God is still our responsibility. The power of God is real and present. Even so, the kingdom of God deals with matters of the greatest importance—our humanity, our ability to see, and our willingness to assist Christ in restoring the human family. Implementation is never easy. Even in the sure presence of the power of God, implementation isn't easy.

It does, however, allow us to rise to the full stature of our humanity. When we take responsibility for recognizing what God wants us to see, for interpreting and understanding our circumstances, and for implementing love, justice, and peace, we are transformed. As with the resurrection, our transformation is finally in the hands of God. Transformation is the effect of God's power. God, however, does not coerce. God doesn't bring us to fulfillment and completion without our consent. The power belongs to God. The responsibility is completely ours.

For Reflection

Who do I know that is in exile? Who has been banished or ostracized? Might Christ be calling on me to find a way to bring that person back into the family or fold? What are the obstacles to restoration? What is the conflict? Where is the friction? How might I help to reduce the friction and make healing possible?

_____

_____

_____

How might I take responsibility for strengthening the family of God? What do I believe should happen? What am I willing to do to initiate transformation and change for the better?

_____

_____

_____

Have I encountered secrecy that is damaging people and relationships? Are there undercurrents, or perhaps even conspiracies? What can I do to open channels of communication and healing?

_____

_____

_____

In both the Supper and in the Garden of Gethsemane, Jesus transforms his own being taken into a gracious gift. What might this mean for my life? What conflicts do I face? What kinds of outcomes are possible if instead of fighting or retaliating, I were to seek to transform the conflict? How might I respond? What are the potential benefits? What are the risks?

_____

_____

_____

Are there important matters that I close my eyes to? Are there people or situations to which I am indifferent? What might it mean for me to open my eyes?

_____

_____

_____

Free Newsletter and Book Offer

BECAUSE OF OUR COMMITMENT to the insights and great ideas that the Gospel of Mark embodies, we have put together an occasional newsletter, which we are pleased to offer you free of charge. Our newsletter is entitled "Families That Thrive." The purpose of the newsletter is to help us learn to recognize the grace that is right before our eyes and to build stronger relationships—both in our families at home and in the larger world of the human family. Many who write newsletters try to get as much money as possible from them. The people of *Families That Thrive* are committed to these ideas and are willing for you to have them free of charge. To register for your free newsletter, we invite you to visit our website, www.familiesthatthrive.com. You can not only register for your newsletter, but you can also visit our archives, where you will have free access to all of our past newsletters.

In addition, to those who purchase *A Whole New World*, we are pleased to offer you an additional bonus. For the price of shipping and handling, $4.95, we will send you a complementary copy of *Walking with the Wise*. In this book, John Blackwell offers more concrete insights into the world of grace in relationships. These are ideas that you can implement in your own relationships today. In addition, there are other words of wisdom in *Walking with the Wise*. Other authors include Chuck Norris, Donald Trump, and

Deepak Chopra. To receive your complementary copy of *Walking with the Wise,* simply go to www.familiesthatthrive.com, and click on *Walking with the Wise* Special Offer.

We also invite you to discover *A Whole New World* on Audio CD and hear John Blackwell shed light on the Gospel of Mark. To order your CDs, simply to go www.morgan-james.com/mark.

John Blackwell has other books that we would like to ask you to purchase. The first volume, *A Whole New World—the Gospel of John,* is available to you. You may purchase this book either from Morgan James or through Families That Thrive. John also has two books published by Crossroad. The first is called *Pride: How Humility and Hospitality Overcome the First Deadly Sin.* The second is entitled *The Noonday Demon.* Both books are full of rich stories and ideas that will enhance your personal growth and fulfillment as a human being. You can order your copies today by logging onto www.familiesthatthrive.com.

Fourth, if you are intrigued by the ideas in *A Whole New World,* why not consider an education at Kansas Wesleyan University. This is a place where you can pursue the kinds of ideas John Blackwell is writing about in greater depth. Kansas Wesleyan University, located in the heart of Kansas, has a warm, friendly, caring faculty. Their love of learning is matched by their love of students. Visit our website: www.kwu.edu.

About the Author

JOHN N. BLACKWELL is Dean of the Chapel at Kansas Wesleyan University, where he also teaches in the departments of Religion and Philosophy, and English. For over thirty years, John has also served as speaker and retreat leader for people of all ages, both in the United States and Europe.

John received his education at San Diego State University, Claremont School of Theology, and Arizona State University, where he earned a Ph.D. in anthropology. John is the author of *A Whole New World—Great Insights into Transformation and Fulfillment from the Gospel of John* (published by Morgan James), *Pride: Identifying and Overcoming the First Deadly Sin*, *The Noonday Demon*, and *The Passion as Story.* He is also a contributor to *Walking with the Wise.* John writes a newsletter for familiesthatthrive.com.

John and his wife, Nancy, make their home in Salina, Kansas. They have two adult children, Jaime, an attorney, and David, a businessman. John enjoys reading, writing, teaching, music, travel, and kite flying.

Acknowledgements

ONE OF MY STUDENTS RECENTLY ASKED ME, "Is writing a book hard?" When I pondered her question, I realized that although writing is sometimes difficult, it is almost always a joy. And for me, publishing a book is joyful in large part because of the collaboration with people who make this possible. Consequently, it is my pleasant duty to thank the people who both play an essential role in the creation of this book and who also give me heart-warming support.

I begin with the talented design team at Morgan James Publishing for their creativity, insight, and spirit. Thank you, David Hancock, Margo Toulouse, Heather Kirk, Norma Strange, Jeanette Barnes, Chris Howard, Cindy Sauer, and Rachel Campbell. Working with you is a pleasure.

I also take pleasure in thanking Philip P. Kerstetter, President of Kansas Wesleyan University. Phil is a great friend. He is a dialogue partner, a mentor, and he makes sure that I have adequate time for study, reflection, and writing. I love my work at Kansas Wesleyan, and having time to reflect and write is the icing on a cake that is already rich and sweet. Moreover, I am blessed with wonderful colleagues and students at Kansas Wesleyan. We have spent many an hour discussing ideas that this book embodies. Because of the people of Kansas Wesleyan University, I am one grateful, happy camper.

I am also grateful to Peter Francis, Warden of St. Deiniol's Library in Wales. St. Deiniol's is a residential library. For me, it's a writer's paradise. This is so not only because of the unique setting of St. Deiniol's, but also because of Peter, his family and staff. They practice the best of hospitality while conducting themselves in a completely professional manner. They embody both the warmth and competence to which they aspire.

My friends Ben and Kathee Christensen, Bonnie Bobzien, and John Mathison, Fellows of the San Diego School of Christian Studies, have also spent many an hour in dialogue over ideas from the Gospel of Mark. I treasure the insights I have gained from their remarkable intelligence, thoughtfulness, and humor.

Kyra Phillips, of CNN in Atlanta, is a wonderful friend who enthusiastically agreed to write the Foreword to this book. Kyra is a skilled journalist who combines principle with courage. I am deeply grateful for both her friendship and her devotion to truth.

Shirley Leggett is a dear friend who gives me seemingly unlimited assistance in the production of our books. I benefit from both her sharp eye (she's a great proofreader) and her feedback. I know of no person who exceeds Shirley's enthusiasm for the learning enterprise. This is what makes her such a great teacher.

I am honored to dedicate this book to my friend and colleague, Jim Standiford, senior pastor of First United Methodist Church, in San Diego. For starters, this man has been listening to the development of my ideas on the Gospel of Mark for a quarter of a century. That in itself is evidence of his immeasurable patience. Jim is fabulous listener. He always gives the person in front of him his undivided, loving attention. Jim's capacity for listening helps his partner in dialogue come to an understanding not only of truth, but also of one's own validity and worth as a human being. I always come away from a conversation with Jim Standiford knowing what it is to be trusted and treasured. The magnitude of his friendship merits far deeper gratitude than one small volume is capable of signifying.

Having thanked Jim, the first shall be last: I thank my family. They have suffered me even longer than Jim has! My wife, Nancy, and our children, Jaime and David, are the treasures with whom I live and move and have my being. Owing to their grace, it is not unusual for our conversation to enter the world of great ideas, including what it means for the world to become new and whole. Sometimes unconsciously, at others, with goodness aforethought, Nancy, Jaime, and Dave have helped me learn to see what is right before my eyes. For me, they are the embodiment of grace. I can never thank them too much.

Also from author John Blackwell

A Whole New World: Great Insights into Transformation and Fulfillment—The Gospel of John (New York: Morgan James Publishing, 2006)

Pride—How Humility and Hospitality Overcome the First Deadly Sin (New York: Crossroad, 2006)

The Noonday Demon: Recognizing and Overcoming the Deadly Sin of Sloth (New York: Crossroad, 2004)

The Passion as Story—The Gospel of Mark (Fortress Press, 1986)

Printed in the USA
CPSIA information can be obtained
at www.ICGtesting.com
JSHW082220140824
68134JS00015B/645